GOLF PLUS

IMPROVING YOUR LIFE
WHILE
ENJOYING YOUR SWING

JIM YOAK

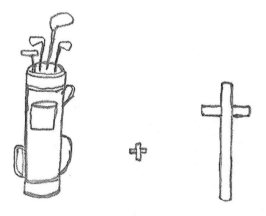

WESTBOW
PRESS®
A DIVISION OF THOMAS NELSON
& ZONDERVAN

Scripture taken from the King James Version of the Bible.

This book is a work of non-fiction. Unless otherwise noted, the author
and the publisher make no explicit guarantees as to the accuracy
of the information contained in this book and in some cases, names
of people and places have been altered to protect their privacy.

Annotations prepared by Henry M. Morris, PhD, LLD, and Litt.D.
President Emeritus, Institute for Creation Research World Publishing.

WestBow Press books may be ordered through booksellers or by contacting:

WestBow Press
A Division of Thomas Nelson & Zondervan
1663 Liberty Drive
Bloomington, IN 47403
www.westbowpress.com
1 (866) 928-1240

Because of the dynamic nature of the Internet, any web addresses or
links contained in this book may have changed since publication and
may no longer be valid. The views expressed in this work are solely those
of the author and do not necessarily reflect the views of the publisher,
and the publisher hereby disclaims any responsibility for them.

Any people depicted in stock imagery provided by Thinkstock are models,
and such images are being used for illustrative purposes only.
Certain stock imagery © Thinkstock.

ISBN: 978-1-5127-5546-6 (sc)
ISBN: 978-1-5127-5547-3 (hc)
ISBN: 978-1-5127-5545-9 (e)

Library of Congress Control Number: 2016914461

Print information available on the last page.

WestBow Press rev. date: 09/08/2016

Contents

Introduction

I started playing golf when I was sixteen years old at the Riverside golf course in Grantsville, West Virginia. In 1965 I was runner-up in the Riverside Open at the little nine-hole hillside golf course. Fifty years later, I still have the trophy that I won. This was the starting point for golf and me. As the years have unfolded, a lot of changes have come about, not only to me but also to the great game of golf. On April 29, 1977, I received Christ as my personal Savior. I continued to play golf and still do today at the age of seventy-one. I firmly believe that when anyone receives Christ by faith and starts following Him scripturally, it will make that one a better person on and off the golf course. After serving as pastor at Faith Baptist Church in Vienna, West Virginia, for twenty years and studying God's word for thirty-eight years, I think it is safe to say that God has given us the Bible that is designed to cause all humankind to see their need for a Savior. It is also full of truths and principles that are a plus for anyone who loves it and is willing to read and study it. It will help in all areas of life, regardless of where we find ourselves.

This book that I am writing is designed to incorporate some truths and principles found in God's word with some of the different aspects of the game of golf. Honestly I don't know how important golf is to God, but from a scriptural point of view, I can say God is interested in the golfer and all others who are made in His image. This book may not improve your swing or lower your score, but I pray it helps you to play, win, lose, watch, and enjoy the game in a new way, and that it might awaken an appetite in you for God's word.

Let's get started!

I Love Golf

I love watching golf on the Golf Channel and other sports networks. I love playing golf. It challenges me and unloads my mind of what is going on outside the golf world for three or four hours. When you hit that sweet spot on the club and the ball is on line and lands on the green close to the pin, that love intensifies. It seems to be very easy to base our love on results. We can attach the word *love* to so many things that it almost becomes a cliché.

A good source of information on love is found in the Bible. It not only reveals how we are to love one another but also portrays our Creator and Redeemer as love. First John 4:7–8 says,

> Beloved, let us love one another: for love is of God; and every one that loveth is born of God, and knoweth God. He that loveth not knoweth not God; for God is love.

As you read and study God's word, you see this love shown throughout its pages. His love is not based on results but is unconditional and universal. It is safe to say we all are recipients of this universal love in a physical and spiritual way. James 1:17 says it best. "Every good gift and every perfect gift is from above, and cometh down from the Father of lights, with whom is no variableness, neither shadow of turning." All sources of good come from this God of love who James designates as the Father of light who never changes.

Roger Benson, pastor at Grace Gospel Church in Pettyville, West Virginia, preached four messages on the most familiar verse that is found in the Bible: John 3:16. In his first message, he talked about the familiar phrase "for God so loved the world." He commented that this is a global love, which I found to be a very true statement. We all live in a world that is very global today.

Golf, over the years, has become a sport that is played, watched, and loved all over the world. There seems to be so much to attach our love to in the world we live in today. It is easy to forget about a global love that was shown when God gave us His only begotten Son. When one believes and receives this greatest gift that was ever given, it can help us to manage, direct, and take love to a new level on and off the golf course.

My little children, let us not love in word,
neither in tongue, but in deed and in truth.
—1 John 3:18

CHAPTER 2

Platforms

Life is full of platforms; some are very rewarding and visible while others are hard and get very little attention. Honestly, from an amateur golfer's perspective, we would all want to be on the platform with those who are blessed to be a part of the PGA and LPGA. Several years ago, platforms were not as visible as they are today. The world is truly watching. In knowing this truth, we need to take advantage of whatever platform we have been given and not allow the platform to take advantage of us.

If we are willing to exercise faith and ask the Lord to stand beside us, this can be a win-win situation—not only for us but also for all others whose eyes are on us. I certainly know it is easy to take for granted what life has entrusted us with. It is easy to get stuck in our own world and forget that we are just a little speck in a great big plan that is unfolding.

From a scripture vantage point, I believe we see our Creator and Savior putting a big puzzle together.

I used to tell the people in the church I pastored to be an important part of this puzzle by exercising your faith in the One who came to give life and give it more abundantly. Faith is the key to being an important part of this plan.

Faith is essential to pleasing God and approaching Him. Hebrews 11:6 says, "But without faith it is impossible to please him: for he that cometh to God must believe that he is, and that he is a rewarder of them that diligently seek him."

A careful study of God's word shows how this faith releases and allows God to reward the believer. Faith is essential if we are going to honor the Lord on the ever-changing platforms of life. If one uses his or her platform wisely, it can make a difference in ways only the Lord knows.

In Colossians 3:23, Paul says, "And whatsoever ye do, do it heartily, as to the Lord, and not unto men." Understand that whatever you are doing, you should do it as if you are doing it for the Lord and not for humanity. If we believe and apply this truth in our lives, it can promote, encourage, provide instruction, and produce contentment in whatever platform you are standing on right now. Time may change the platform, but unwavering faith in Christ is rewarded in life as well as in death.

According to my earnest expectation and my hope,
that in nothing I shall be ashamed, but that with
all boldness, as always, so now also Christ shall be
magnified in my body, whether it be by life, or by
death. For to me to live is Christ, and to die is gain.
—Philippians 1:20–21

CHAPTER 3

The Practice Range

My wife and I were blessed to attend one day at the Greenbrier Open in White Sulphur Springs, West Virginia. It was there that we first got to see some of the golfers preparing on the practice range before starting their rounds. To professional golfers and serious amateurs, this is an important part of the game. The driving range or practice range is so important if one plans to be in the winner's circle. Someone once said if you fail to plan, plan on failing. It seems as if humanity has been given the ability and technology in the sports world that allows the athlete to be successful. But the responsibility still lies at the feet of those who choose to use it or not. The resources to be successful in our great country seem to be numerous, in the physical realm as well as the spiritual realm, if we incorporate them into our lives.

The Bible is such a valuable resource for life. I have said many times in my years as a pastor that the Bible is a book that will show you how to live a good life and die a good death. It is safe to say that it is a book about preparation. Paul's words certainly echoed this truth about the scriptures in what he wrote in 2 Timothy 3:16–17.

> All scripture is given by inspiration of God, and is profitable for doctrine, for reproof, for correction, for instruction in righteousness: That the man of God may be perfect, thoroughly furnished unto all good works.

Paul saw the scripture as being profitable or useful. It is profitable for teaching, correcting, convicting, and instructing one in righteousness. He understood this would make one complete or mature while equipping the reader and doer unto all good works.

A good way to prepare for the day ahead is to look into the perfect law of liberty and continue therein, being not a forgetful hearer but a doer of the work. James 1:25 says this man or person shall be blessed in his deeds. This will add a new dimension to one's life. Omitting the instruction found in God's word results in lives that are out of balance. Just as the practice range prepares us for the game of golf, God's word prepares us for the game of life. Spending a little time daily in the Bible is a practice that pays great dividends.

> Study to shew thyself approved unto God,
> a workman that needeth not to be ashamed,
> rightly dividing the word of truth.
> —2 Timothy 2:15

CHAPTER 4

The First Tee

There always seems to be a degree of anxiety on the first tee. The anxiety level rises in knowing that all eyes are on you. The result of that first shot can build confidence and affect the rest of the game. We all have a tendency to forget how important first things are in life. One of the ways Webster's dictionary defines *first* is "ranking above all others in importance or quality."

In the golf world, there is an organization that is called the First Tee. It is designed to impact the lives of young people by providing educational programs that "build character, instill life-changing values, and promote healthy choices through the game of golf," according to the First Tee website. I always enjoy listening to the First Tee commentators on TV, as they share what those children and young people have to say. I do not know who came up with this idea, but it sure seems to be making a difference in the lives of many young people.

In the physical world, first things are so important—first child, first step, first school day, first job, first paycheck, first car, and first win.

In the spiritual world, the Bible is a good source of information about firsts. Genesis is the first book and is all about beginnings. In this book, we are introduced to the first man, Adam, and the first woman, Eve. We even see the first sin or the act of disobeying God. Likewise, we see the first act of rescue or redeeming humankind by God who created man and woman in His own image. This act of salvation required blood to be shed. Many Bible scholars believe the first blood shed in God's great redemptive plan was in the Garden of Eden, when God made coats of skins and clothed Adam and Eve. Genesis 3:21 says, "Unto Adam also and to his wife did the Lord God make coats of skins, and clothed them." A footnote in my Bible on this verse says,

> This action is very instructive in several ways: (1) God considers clothes so vital in this present world that He Himself provided it for our first parents; (2) the aprons fashioned by Adam and Eve were inadequate, testifying in effect that man-made efforts to prepare for God's presence will be rejected; (3) the clothing provided by God required shedding the blood of two animals, probably two sheep, who were thus the first creatures actually to suffer death after Adam's

sin, illustrating the basic biblical principle of substitutionary atonement (or "covering"), requiring the shedding of innocent blood as a condition of forgiveness for the sinner."[1]

Throughout the pages of God's word, we see a program that was set forth that required innocent blood to be shed to make atonement for humankind. The first sin led to the first acts of redemption and atonement that would find fulfillment in the incarnation, the embodiment of God in the human form of Jesus.

The first book in the New Testament gives us the account of God coming to us in the person of Jesus Christ. Matthew 1:23 tells us of this supernatural event where a virgin would be with child and bring forth a Son and call Him Emmanuel, which is interpreted as "God with us." Matthew 1:21, tells why God came to be with us. It was to save His people from their sins. Adam, the first man, brought sin, but God, who loved us, first brought salvation and life through His Son, whom Paul designated in 2 Corinthians 15:45 as the last Adam, who was made a quickening spirit.

As important as getting off to a good start on the first tee, maybe this chapter has reminded or raised the awareness of just how important firsts are in the physical realm as well as in the spiritual.

Therefore take no thought, saying, What shall we eat? or, What shall we drink? or, Wherewithal shall we be clothed? (For after all these things do the Gentiles seek:) for your heavenly Father knoweth that ye have need of all these things. But seek ye first the kingdom of God, and his righteousness; and all these things shall be added unto you.

—Matthew 6:31–33

CHAPTER 5

The Beauty of the Beast

While writing this chapter, I have been watching the Hyundai Tournament of Champions being played on the western shores in Maui, Hawaii. The beauty of this course and the scenery surrounding it is breathtaking. I heard one announcer talking about how it must be hard to stay focused while being surrounded by the beautiful view. Sometimes in the golf world, the way we play may not be beautiful and the difficulty in getting pars or birdies may make the course seem like a beast. But overall, golf reflects a beauty in the men and women that play it, in dress, character, speech, and sportsmanship. In all my years of playing and watching, I have never seen a fight break out on the golf course. This beauty is not only seen in the people who play but also in the courses that are being played on all over the world.

There is a degree of entertainment in things that are beautiful. Watching golf being played in beautiful places is entertaining. Watching all the different birds and the black and gray squirrels on the snow-covered ground here in West Virginia is also very entertaining to my wife and me. I tell my wife it is free entertainment.

Things beautiful are not only entertaining but there is also a message in beauty that radiates out day and night for all to see. David, the sweet psalmist, wrote in Psalm 19:1–3,

> The heavens declare the glory of God; and the firmament sheweth his handiwork. Day unto day uttereth speech, and night unto night sheweth knowledge. There is no speech nor language, where their voice is not heard.

When you go outside and look up, whether it is day or night, do not think of it as just an empty space. It is a revelation from God and a proclamation of His handiwork. This message or revelation continues day and night. It is like God has done His part in revealing Himself through creation. Man-made beauty is very temporal. We have all heard the familiar phrase "Beauty is only skin-deep." That statement probably has a temporal connotation to it as well as an outward connotation.

More than once, I have seen golf courses that were certainly beautiful go out of business and soon their beauty was gone. The beauty that we all enjoy and sometimes take for granted goes far beyond that made by man.

The next time you are enjoying the beautiful outdoors, whether on the golf course or off, take time to look, listen, and learn of the One who does so much more for us than we can do for ourselves.

He hath made everything beautiful in his time: also
he hath set the world in their heart,
so that no man can find out the work that
God maketh from the beginning to the end.
—Ecclesiastes 3:11

CHAPTER 6

Uniqueness

I have always felt that golf is a unique game. Its uniqueness is shown in a public way as well as a personal way. The public can now see the best golfers playing all over the world in a sport where the lowest numbers win, not the highest. This uniqueness is shown most in a personal way. The late and great Payne Stewart was unique in the way he dressed and played the game. Rickie Fowler is unique in these same ways today. It is also shown in swing patterns and the way one approaches the ball. I love to watch the way Keegan Bradley addresses the ball. His concentration and repetition are great.

Uniqueness, I believe, was in the mind of God when He created humankind. It is mind-boggling to think everybody has a different fingerprint. When you read and study the Old Testament in the Bible, you see how God brought the nation of Israel into being. They were designed to be a unique people. Deuteronomy 14:2 says, "For thou art an holy people unto the Lord thy

God, and the Lord hath chosen thee to be a peculiar people unto himself, above all the nations that are upon the earth."

Later in the New Testament, Peter would use this Old Testament terminology to describe the New Testament believer. He said in 1 Peter 2:9, "But ye are a chosen generation, a royal priesthood, an holy nation, a peculiar people; that ye should shew forth the praises of him who hath called you out of darkness into marvelous light."

The Old Testament responsibilities, to be unique, have been transferred to the New Testament Christian. We are to be a peculiar people, a special possession that would praise the Lord who has called us out of darkness into His marvelous light.

Uniqueness that makes a positive contribution to life is so valuable. Those that first started following Christ were taught to be the salt of the earth and the light of the world. Salt preserves, and light dispels darkness. Biblical uniqueness is such a needed element today, in a world that is so full of sin and darkness.

The same way one's individual uniqueness gets attention and makes a difference in the physical realm, a spiritual uniqueness pleases the Lord and is so needed at work or at play.

Be ye not unequally yoked together with unbelievers: for what fellowship hath righteousness with unrighteousness? and what communion hath light with darkness? And what concord hath Christ with Belial? or what part hath he that believeth with an infidel? And what agreement hath the temple of God with idols? for ye are the temple of the living God; as God hath said, I will dwell in them, and walk in them; and I will be their God, and they shall be my people. Wherefore come out from among them, and be ye separate, saith the Lord and touch not the unclean thing; and I will receive you, And will be a Father unto you, and ye shall be my sons and daughters, saith the Lord God Almighty.

—2 Corinthians 6:14–18

CHAPTER 7

Looking Up

I suppose one of the first things that I heard while learning to play golf was "Keep your head down. Don't look up." When I ignore this basic element of golf, it seems I top or maybe blade the ball, which only spells disaster on my scorecard.

Learned behavior on the golf course can be challenging but very rewarding. This means I have to remind myself of some of these simple techniques as I play the game. Staying focused on what is at hand is another aspect of the game that is very important, especially when you are just out to have a good time in the beauty of the outdoors.

I have realized after playing this game for many years that there is so much more to golf than winning or shooting a good score. Just think how much more there is to see and enjoy on a golf course than being in a crowded coliseum or football stadium. I guess this is an opinion of one who loves the outdoors and is not fond of big crowds.

From my perspective as an old, worn-out golfer, I know there is a bad side to looking up when it comes to golf but a good side when it comes to life. I guess what I am trying to say is that there is so much more to see in life than what the eye beholds. Chuck Swindoll, one of my favorite authors, says it best in his book titled *Growing Strong in the Seasons of Life.* In the summer section of this book, he writes about insight. He says,

Are you ready for a surprise? You blink twenty-five times every minute. Each blink takes you about one-fifth of a second. Therefore, if you take a ten-hour automobile trip, averaging forty miles per hour, you will drive twenty miles with your eyes closed. I know a fact far more surprising than that. Some people go through life with their eyes closed. They look but do not really "see" ... They observe the surface but omit the underneath ... They focus on images but not issues ... Vision is present but perception is absent. If life were a painting, they would see colors but no genius in the strokes of the brush. If it were a journey, they would notice a road but no majestic, awesome scenery. If it were a meal, they would eat and drink but overlook the exquisite beauty of the china and the delicate touch of wine in the sauce. If it were a poem, they would read print on the page but miss altogether the passion of the poet. Remove insight and you suddenly reduce life to existence with frequent flashes of boredom and indifference.[2]

I believe if insight, which my dictionary defines as "the capacity to discern the true nature of a situation," exists, it can only add a new dimension to a fuller life. It, like so many other things on or off the golf course, is a learned behavior.

I believe a good starting point for cultivating insight is God's word. The Bible asks us to look beyond situations and look to the one that controls them. In light of Paul being troubled on every side, he writes these encouraging and insightful words to the church at Corinth in 2 Corinthians 4:16–18:

For which cause we faint not; but though our outward man perish, yet the inward man is renewed day by day. For our light affliction, which is but for a moment, worketh for us a far more exceeding and eternal weight of glory. While we look not at the things which are seen but at the things which are not seen: for the things which are seen are temporal; but the things which are not seen are eternal.

Because of his faith in Christ, Paul was able to see beyond the situation. He saw all the affliction as momentary compared to the unseen things, which are eternal.

When the outlook seems grim, try the uplook. Better yet, if you believe and realize all sources of good come from our maker's hand, don't wait for the bad times but look up daily to that help which made the heavens and the earth. Psalm 121:1–2 says it best. "I will lift up mine eyes unto the hills, from whence cometh my help. My help cometh from the Lord, which made heaven and earth."

The help that all humankind needs the most came down from heaven, namely Jesus Christ. Christ's words echo this truth in John 6:32–33.

> Then Jesus said unto them, Verily, verily, I say unto you, Moses gave you not that bread from heaven; but my Father giveth you the true bread from heaven. For the bread of God is he which cometh down. and giveth life unto the world.

The point is that the true bread that came down from heaven was the God-Man that is capable of giving life abundantly and eternally. This life can satisfy spiritual hunger and thirst. There is so much to look at in this world, which can be detrimental to an uplook if we allow it. I trust we all may keep our heads down on the golf course but that in life we lift our eyes "from whence cometh my help."

> My voice shall thou hear in the
> morning, O Lord; in the morning will I
> direct my prayer unto thee, and look up.
> —Psalm 5:3

CHAPTER 8

Playing by the Rules

I know that the rulebook is an important part to those that have been blessed to play on the PGA and LPGA. How important is this book to these men and women? It can mean winning, losing, or being disqualified. We have probably all heard the expression "Rules are made to be broken." Believing these words can lead to behaviors or actions that can be very costly personally and publicly.

Breaking the rules can have a twofold effect. During my years working at DuPont Washington Works in Wood County, West Virginia, I soon learned that safety rules were an important part of the job. As important as the rulebook is in golf or the workplace, there is another book of rules that one needs to consider.

The Bible is a book of rules that are expressed as commands or commandments. Very early in this book, we not only see rules established but also rules broken. Genesis 2:16–17, says,

And the Lord God commanded the man, saying, Of every tree of the garden thou mayest freely eat: But of the tree of the knowledge of good and evil, thou shalt not eat of it: for in the day that thou eatest thereof thou shalt surely die.

A footnote in my Bible on these verses says,

The restriction imposed here by God is the simplest, most straightforward test that could be devised for determining man's volitional response to God's love. There was only one minor restraint placed on Adam's freedom, and with an abundance of delicious fruit of all types available, there was no justification for his desiring the one forbidden fruit. Nevertheless, he did have a choice, and so he was a free moral agent capable of accepting or rejecting God's will.[1]

Choice certainly comes into play when it comes to rules. It can affect not only us but others also.

In relationship to this act of disobedience by the first man, Paul said in Romans 5:12, "Wherefore, as by one man sin entered into the world, and death by sin; and so death passed upon all men, for that all have sinned." The one man Paul talks about in this verse is none other than Adam. The good news is there is another man that came to this earth who was God in the flesh and who truly played by the rules. If you are willing to see yourself, see your need for this Savior, and follow Him scripturally, I believe you can start playing by a new set of rules that can add a new dimension to your life as well as influence others that may be following in your footsteps.

And let the peace of God rule in your hearts, to the which also ye are called in one body; and be ye thankful. Let the word of Christ dwell in you richly in all wisdom; teaching and admonishing one another in psalms and hymns and spiritual songs, singing with grace in your hearts to the Lord. And whatsoever ye do in word or deed, do all in the name of the Lord Jesus, giving thanks to God and the Father by him.
—Colossians 3:15–17

CHAPTER 9

Competition

A competitive spirit can clearly be seen on and off the golf course. It is very visible, not only in the sports world but in the business world as well. It seems to be a driving force in this world we are a part of and seems to extend even beyond the human realm to the natural realm. I so enjoy sitting on the front porch in the summertime while watching the little hummingbirds competing against each other for that sweet water in the feeder. It is certainly safe to say that competition has an entertaining element to it. Competition can almost become brutal in some sports. I suppose that is the reason I enjoy golf more than any other sport or game.

The Webster dictionary describes competition as "the act of competing as for profit or a prize." A lot of hard work seems to go along with those that profit in competing. This work not only seems to profit them personally but also profits so many others through the generosity that is shown in the golf world.

Life seems to be full of learned behaviors as well as natural behaviors. It is natural for newborns to cry when they are hungry. It is not natural for young children to say thank-you unless they have been taught. When it comes to competing, perhaps both play a role.

I think it is safe to say there can be a good side and a bad side to competition. I believe if we are only competing for the prizes and profits in this world, our life is somewhat out of balance.

Paul, who wrote most of the books in the New Testament, uses the example of an athlete competing in a race to encourage the believer to put a lot into their walk with the Lord. Paul says in 1 Corinthians 9:24–27,

> Know ye not that they which run in a race run all, but one receiveth the prize? So run, that ye may obtain. And every man that striveth for the mastery is temperate in all things. Now they do it to obtain a corruptible crown; but we an incorruptible. I therefore so run, not as uncertainly; so fight I, not as one that beateth the air: But I keep under my body, and bring it into subjection: lest that by any means, when I have preached to others, I myself should be a castaway.

In this race, we see the need to put a lot into it, namely self-control and a willingness to submit or obey. We see one competing for a perishable crown and one competing for an imperishable crown.

Paul understood and saw the competitive spirit in the sports world of that day, but he also understood that same determination was so needed in the spiritual world. I believe the spiritual race can give a new face to all the other races in life that can help us compete in an honorable way.

Brethren, I count not myself to have apprehended; but this one thing I do, forgetting those things which are behind, and reaching forth unto those things which are before, I press toward the mark for the prize of the high calling of God in Christ Jesus.
—Philippians 3:13–14

CHAPTER 10

Laugh It Off

Being able to laugh off a bad shot and let it go is probably a plus for your game, as well as those you are playing with. I always enjoy seeing laughter and happiness as I watch golf, whether it is between the players, players and fans, or the players and caddies. This makes this great game of golf even greater. Laughter is an element that helps keep things in perspective and has a therapeutic quality about it.

I heard it said a long time ago that what makes you laugh says a lot about you. I think there is a lot to be learned from this statement. In the entertainment and advertising world, we see some things that are worth laughing about and some that are not. Anyone who has ever been laughed at or made fun of would certainly say that not every thing is funny.

Laughter, like so many other things, seems to be built into the makeup of humankind and certainly needs spiritual help to manage it. Proverbs 15:13 says, "A merry heart maketh a cheerful countenance: but by sorrow of the heart the spirit is broken." Laughter, at its best, expresses a joyful or a merry heart. Joy is expressed outwardly. You can see it on one's face. The emotional condition of a person can affect the body and the spirit.

In Proverbs 17:22, we also see that "a merry heart doeth good like medicine: But a broken spirit drieth the bones." The word *merry* in this proverb is taken from a Hebrew word that means "to be gleeful, glad, or rejoice."

There is apparently a great benefit to this psychological makeup. This makeup can foster good health or it is like good medicine.

No wonder Paul, who wrote most of the books in the New Testament, so often talks about rejoicing or joy. From a scripture point of view, laughter is a timed event. Ecclesiastes 3:4 says there is a time to weep and a time to laugh. May I say, in closing, this chapter allows your laughter to brighten up, benefit, and make a better world.

Rejoice evermore. Pray without ceasing.
In every thing give thanks: for this is the will of
God in Christ Jesus concerning you.
—1 Thessalonians 5:16–18

CHAPTER 11

Humility

I think it is safe to say the game of golf can humble oneself. The good news is that humility is often seen in this game. I do not think I have ever seen a player going around sticking up their finger indicating they are number one. I have seen players on television, with the world watching, being very complimentary and almost apologetic to the other player they have just beaten. This not only leaves a good taste in the mouth of those watching, but it also shows a quality that is so needed in our society.

Honestly, I feel pride is probably one of the worst enemies of humility. A woman came to her pastor and told him she was dealing with pride. She said, "Every time I look in the mirror, I think I am the most beautiful woman in the world." The pastor looked at her and said, "That is not pride. That is a mistake." As humorous as this is, visible humility is a welcoming sight.

Life is so full of thoughts, feelings, and emotions that we all need a source of information that can help counteract these mental attitudes. The Bible can be that source, if one is willing to use it. Within this book, you see some of the writers of the New Testament encouraging the readers to humble themselves, but you can also see the ultimate example of humility: Jesus Christ. Peter, who was one of the disciples of Christ, wrote in 1 Peter 5:5–6,

> Likewise, ye younger, submit yourselves unto the elder. Yea, all of you be subject one to another, and be clothed with humility: for God resisteth the proud, and giveth grace to the humble. Humble yourselves therefore under the mighty hand of God, that he may exalt you in due time.

God's word teaches us to relinquish our own rights. We humble ourselves by doing this. Humility, in the Bible, simply means assuming the role that God has assigned to us in life. It is synonymous with submission, and this is the starting point for being clothed in humility. If one assumes this role, we can expect God to exalt us in His time.

Jesus Christ was the supreme example of being clothed in humility. Paul said it best in Philippians 2:5–9.

> Let this mind be in you, which was also in Christ Jesus: Who, being in the form of God, thought it not robbery to be equal with God; But made

himself of no reputation, and took upon him the form of a servant, and was made in the likeness of men: And being found in fashion as a man, he humbled himself, and became obedient unto death, even the death of the cross. Wherefore God also hath highly exalted him, and given him a name which is above every name.

In these verses, Paul is asking the believer to have the mind of Christ. The mind of Christ was not about a reputation but about serving, humility, and obedience. Christ took this to a new level and left us an example that we should follow in His steps.

Wherever you find yourself in life, humility is a very refreshing thing. It is a positive addition to anyone's life that speaks very loudly without words.

At the same time came the disciples unto Jesus, saying, Who is the greatest in the kingdom of heaven? And Jesus called a little child unto him, and set him in the midst of them, And said, Verily I say unto you, Except ye be converted, and become as little children, ye shall not enter into the kingdom of heaven. Whosoever therefore shall humble himself as this little child, the same is greatest in the kingdom of heaven. And whoso shall receive one such little child in my name receiveth me.
—Matthew 18:1–5

CHAPTER 12

Identifying

If the amateur golfer is honest, we would all like to be able to hit the ball the way the men and women do on the professional level. It is easier for us to identify with an occasional bad shot they may make than all the good ones they consistently make. The Webster dictionary defines *identifying* as "associating or affiliating oneself closely with a person or group."

There are so many more things to identify with in this world today than there was when I started playing golf more than fifty years ago. Some are good and some are bad. Wherever we are in life, we all should stop and consider that someone is identifying with us. It may be our dress, speech, or behavior. Several years ago, while driving my car on a trip through another county in West Virginia, I saw this big man and little boy walking down through the yard from a farmhouse. The big man had on a pair of coveralls and gum boots. The little boy, probably four years old, was dressed the same way, just following him along. Identifying comes into play in all walks of life and certainly starts in the family setting.

I remember a year or two ago one of my golfing buddies found a golf ball that had three crosses on it as an identification mark. It was not only a blessing to see this, but as a Christian, I could identify with this because it took a cross and a death to provide salvation and deliverance for humankind. It is hard to wrap our minds around how God, our Creator, became a man in the person of Jesus Christ and was willing to go to a cross and die for us so we could have forgiveness and the promise of everlasting life.

One of the greatest demonstrations of identification is echoed in John 1:14–17.

> And the Word was made flesh, and dwelt among us, and (we beheld his glory, the glory as of the only begotten of the Father) full of grace and truth, John bare witness of him and cried, saying, This was he of whom I spake, He that cometh after me is preferred before me: for he was before me. And of his fulness have all we received, and grace for grace. For the law was given by Moses, but grace and truth came by Jesus Christ.

The footnote in my study Bible for verse 14 says, "This is the great verse of the incarnation, when the eternal Word took on human flesh." This verse and the following verses unequivocally refer to "Jesus Christ" (1:17), so there is no legitimate escape (though many have tried) from the great truth that Jesus was the great God and Creator, as well as a perfect man and redeeming Savior. Furthermore, He has assumed human flesh forever while still remaining fully God. He is not part man and part God, or sometimes man and sometimes God, but is now and eternally the God-Man. He is fully and always true God and perfect man—man as God created and intended man to be.[1]

As you study the life of this God-Man, you see one that fully identified with the God of the universe as well as fallen humanity. The writer of Hebrews portrays this God-Man as a high priest that has associated himself with us. Hebrews 4:14–16 says,

> Seeing then that we have a great high priest, that is passed into the heavens, Jesus the Son of God, let us hold fast our profession. For we have not an high priest which cannot be touched with the feeling of our infirmities; but was in all points tempted like as we are, yet without sin. Let us therefore come boldly unto the throne of grace, that we may obtain mercy, and find grace to help in time of need.

The God-Man knows our human condition, he experienced our experiences, and he knows our weakness, so he can sympathize with us. He did all this apart from sin. This kind of Savior and high priest should give the believer boldness to come to him for mercy and grace in time of need.

God's word is full of good options to identify with if we choose to do so. We all know in the world today it seems nothing is hidden. This alone takes the power of identity to a new level. This ought to raise the awareness that someone is watching and someone may identify with what they are watching.

Now also when I am old and greyheaded,
O God,
forsake me not; until I have shewed thy
strength
unto this generation, and thy power
to every one that is to come.
—Psalm 71:18

CHAPTER 13

Hole in One

You can play and enjoy this game of golf all your life and never experience this milestone. I remember playing at South Hills several years ago and on the third hole, which was a short par three, I was six inches from reaching this milestone. Not too long ago, I read in the paper where Tom Waldron, a coworker and brother in Christ, made a hole-in-one on this hole. Congratulations, Tom! Anyone who really enjoys this game, regardless of his or her playing skills, can always look forward to the next hole with anticipation.

Expectation and anticipation are what make the game of golf so enjoyable and they foster hope in one's life. The Webster dictionary defines *hope* as "to wish for something with expectation of it being fulfilled."

Our physical abilities and God-given talents certainly foster hope. Therefore, hope plays an important role in progressing or moving forward. We need to be like a turtle. The only way he progresses or moves forward is when he sticks his neck out. I believe hope is far more than just wishing for something with expectation.

The apostle Paul wrote to the Christians at Ephesus and reminded them that at one time they were without hope. He said in Ephesians 2:11–14,

> Wherefore remember, that ye being in time past Gentiles in the flesh, who are called Uncircumcision by that which is called the Circumcision in the flesh made by hands; That at that time ye were without Christ, being aliens from the commonwealth of Israel, and strangers from the covenants of promise, having no hope, and without God in the world: But now in Christ Jesus ye who sometimes were far off are made nigh by the blood of Christ. For he is our peace, who hath made both one, and hath broken down the middle wall of partition between us.

Paul, in these verses, wants these Gentile believers to remember that at one time they were aliens and not participants. They had no part in the Jewish community. They were strangers from the covenants of promise and were without hope without God in the world.

However, the good news is Paul also wants them to remember that barrier that separated the Jew and Gentile has been broken down. Paul certainly knew that Jesus Christ was the answer because He gives hope. He also can take the hopeless and give them hope. There are many things in life that can foster hope, and that is okay. But there is also a hope that can be found and experienced when one is willing to experience faith in the death, burial, and resurrection of Jesus Christ. This gives hope a new meaning and takes it to a new level.

I hope you can make a hole-in-one before your golfing days are over. But most of all, I hope that you are looking for that blessed hope and the glorious appearing of the great God and our Savior: Jesus Christ.

Wherein God, willing more abundantly to shew
unto the heirs of promise the immutability
of his counsel, confirmed it by an oath.
That by two immutable things,
in which it was impossible for God to lie,
we might have a strong consolation,
who have fled for refuge to lay hold
upon the hope set before us;
Which hope we have as an anchor of the soul,
both sure and steadfast,
and which entereth into that within the veil.
—Hebrews 6:17–19

CHAPTER 14

Feeding the Fairway

To maintain the beauty and health of the golf course, I am sure lots of money and time are spent on fertilizer, water, and aeration to keep the course in top condition. Feeding plays a major role in the nature world. Humankind is an important instrument in the process. We all can take for granted the men and women that grow, process, and provide the food that is such a necessity for survival. My wife, Darlene, was always a stay-at-home mom. I have such good memories of coming home from work and she would have a good meal cooked. At the time, I may have taken that for granted, but now it is one of the many appreciative memories I have. She has always done a good job in feeding her family.

There is a miraculous element also when it comes to feeding. Being an outdoorsman, I sure can see all the food that is provided for the animal world, and man has nothing to with it.

As a pastor, I always thought one of my greatest responsibilities was to feed the flock. Before that could happen, I had to feed on God's word. Paul put it this way in Romans 10:17: "So then faith cometh by hearing, and hearing by the word of God." Faith always has an object. Make no mistake about it: the God of the Old Testament, who is the Savior of the New Testament, is the object of our biblical faith. The results of faith measure its validity. James 2:17–18 says,

> Even so faith, if it hath not works, is dead, being alone. Yea, a man may say, Thou hast faith, and I have works: shew me thy faith without thy works, and I will shew thee my faith by my works.

The reality or realness of faith is demonstrated or validated by one's work.

In January 2015, Sammy Fry from North Carolina spoke at Grace Gospel Church in Pettyville. He centered all of his messages around our walk with God. In the first message, he taught about demonic faith versus dynamic faith. Demonic faith is seen in James 2:19. "Thou believest that there is one God; thou doest well: the devils also believe, and tremble." Demonic faith believes there is one God, but this is far from dynamic faith that is shown by their work.

I read on Amazon.com excerpts from a book, *Faith in the Fairway,* written by some of the professional golfers. It was kind of testimonials of how important God and His word are to them. It was blessing to me and spoke just how important faith is on and off the golf course.

Biblical faith asks us to do things sometimes that do not seem to make sense. The story is told of a man that fell off a rock cliff. As he was falling, he reached out and grabbed a little bush growing out of the cleft in the rock. He was hanging on, looking straight up, and yelled at the top of his voice, "Is there anybody up there?" A voice from heaven said yes. He yelled, "Can you help me?" A voice from heaven said yes. The man yelled, "What do you want me to do?" The voice from heaven said, "Let go." The man yelled, "Is there anyone *else* up there?" The more we feed our faith, the more we can let go of things that stunt our spiritual growth.

In the game of golf and other sports, I have heard it said that we feed off each other. In the spiritual world, we need to do likewise. Feeding your faith or adding to it will starve so many things that are detrimental to your spiritual growth. In the same way feeding is so vital to giving life to the grass and vegetation on a golf course, faith is so vital to the spiritual life that God's word offers to all who choose to believe.

And beside this, giving all diligence,
add to your faith virtue; and to virtue knowledge;
And to knowledge temperance; and to temperance
patience; and to patience godliness;

And to godliness brotherly kindness and to
brotherly kindness charity. For if these things
be in you, and abound, they make you that
ye shall neither
be barren nor unfruitful in the knowledge
of our Lord Jesus Christ.
—2 Peter 1:5–8

CHAPTER 15

Improving Your Lie

Sometimes in really wet conditions, the professional golfer is allowed to pick up the ball and clean it then lay it back down. As amateur golfers playing golf in West Virginia and Ohio, my friends and I have an agreement. We can improve our lie without a penalty stroke. We call it winter rules, and this sure helps us enjoy the game more.

Anything that can help improve our life or the lives of others is certainly an asset as long as it is not harmful to others. Even as I am writing this book, I am doing it the old-fashioned way with a pen and paper. My wife of fifty-one years will put it on the computer for me. I am guilty as many others are who never take advantage of all the resources that are available to make life better.

There is another source that I believe we all need to take advantage of: God's word. This book is so much about improvement. It is a book that can help us play the game of life by a new set of rules. It certainly can go against the grain of what the world teaches or what the old fallen nature of humankind tries to promote. It can help us maintain a balance in life that not only improves personally but publicly.

I would be very inadequate to try to talk about, comment, purchase, and possess all the things that are available today to make one a better golfer. It is almost mind-boggling when we realize all the improvements that have materialized over the last one hundred years in this great country that we live in. I had the privilege to minister to a man by the name of Howard Lott. He was a member and deacon in the church I pastored. He died on August 8, 2013, at the age of 106. Every time I was around this man, I could not help but to think of all the changes he had seen in those 106 years. Howard was a recipient and witness to many improvements in life. He had understood, many years ago, how God's word is about improvement. What I am trying to say in this chapter is that improving your lie in golf gives you an advantage. Likewise, the principles and teaching of God's word, when received and valued, improve life.

God's word calls for us to love without pretense. Romans 12:9 says, "Let love be without dissimulation. Abhor that which is evil; cleave to that which is good."

God's word calls for us to forgive and pray for others. Luke 6:27–28 says, "But I say unto you which hear, Love your enemies, do good to them which hate you, Bless them that curse you, and pray for them which despitefully use you."

God's word calls for us to relinquish our own rights. Matthew 5:41 says, "And whosoever shall compel thee to go a mile, go with him twain."

God's word calls for us to value others and seek their good. Philippians 2:3–4, says, "Let nothing be done through strife or vainglory; but in lowliness of mind let each esteem other better than themselves. Look not every man on his own things, but every man also on the things of others."

The more we can utilize or apply the principles found in God's word, the more we can improve life. Amen.

Let the word of Christ dwell in you richly in
all wisdom; teaching and admonishing one another
in psalms and hymns and spiritual songs,
singing with grace in your hearts to the Lord.
And whatsoever ye do in word or deed, do all in
the name of the Lord Jesus,
giving thanks to God and the Father by him.
—Colossians 3:16–17

CHAPTER 16

Exercise

One of the many things I like about golf is it is a good source of exercise. This is the kind of exercise that I could do almost daily if I had the time, money, and my wife's approval. There are numerous golf jokes that are told. This is one of my favorites: "I am sick and tired of being left alone every weekend," grumbled the golf widow. "If you think you are going to play today, you have another think coming." "Nonsense," replied the husband, reaching for the toast. "Golf is the farthest thing from my mind. Now could you please pass the putter?"[3]

Exercise is so much more enjoyable if there is a fun element to it. For years, I have tried to work out a few minutes each day in my garage and then walk four miles. This outdoor walk is the favorite part of my exercise. I so enjoy all the outdoor activity I encounter during this time.

I believe it is hard to separate exercise and discipline. Being disciplined can surely be about punishment, but it is also about controlling one's behavior to obtain a certain result. It is so hard to discipline ourselves. When you look at those in the PGA, LPGA, and all others in the sports world, you can see clearly the relationship between exercise and discipline. This is a winning combination in the physical realm as well as the spiritual realm. From a scriptural point of view, we see the word *exercise* being used in relationship to things that are hard to understand.

Psalm 131:1 says, "Lord, my heart is not haughty, nor mine eyes lofty: neither do I exercise myself in great matters or in things too high for me." We see it being used in relationship to the Lord showing lovingkindness, judgment, and righteousness. Jeremiah 9:23–24 says,

> Thus saith the Lord, Let not the wise man glory in his wisdom, neither let the mighty man glory in his might, let not the rich man glory in his riches: But let him that glorieth glory in this, that he understand and knoweth me, that I am the Lord which exercise lovingkindness, judgment and righteousness, in the earth: for in these things I delight, saith the Lord.

We see it in relationship to authority. Jesus said in Matthew 20:25–28,

> But Jesus called them unto him, and said, Ye know that the princes of the Gentiles exercise

dominion over them, and they that are great exercise authority upon them. But it shall not be so among you: but whosoever will be great among you, let him be your minister; And whosoever will be chief among you, let him be your servant: Even as the Son of man came not to be ministered unto, but to minister, and to give his life a ransom for many.

We also see it used in relationship to godliness in 1 Timothy 4:7–9.

But refuse profane and old wives' fables, and exercise thyself rather unto godliness. For bodily exercise profited little: but godliness is profitable unto all things, having promise of the life that now is, and of which is to come.

We seem to live in a world that puts a lot of emphasis on exercise. I certainly cannot comprehend all the effort, energy, and money that is invested in the exercising world. However, I am concerned that not enough time is spent on exercising ourselves unto godliness.

In closing this chapter, let me say to us all, "Do not allow something important to overshadow or destroy something more important. Working out daily in God's word is profitable in all things and promotes a well-balanced life."

This book of the law shall not
depart out of thy mouth;
but thou shalt meditate therein day and night,
that thou mayest observe
to do according to all that is written therein;
for then thou shalt make thy way prosperous,
and then thou shalt have good success.
—Joshua 1:8

CHAPTER 17

Mental Fog

I have heard this term used in relationship to playing golf. I believe it is all about losing focus, which can lead to bad decisions. Keeping one's mind focused on what is ahead can be very trying. In my years of reading and studying the Bible, I personally have experienced this many times. It is so hard to control the mind.

Many years ago, I read a book written by Chuck Swindoll titled *Come before Winter and Share My Hope*. One of the stories in this book was about Sunday Listening. In that chapter, he said,

> Most of us were born hearing well, but all of us must learn to listen well. Listening is a skill, an art that is in need of being cultivated. Dr. Ralph Nichols, considered by many to be an authority on the subject, believes that we think four, perhaps five times faster than we talk. This means that if a speaker utters one hundred twenty words a minute, the audience thinks at about five

hundred words a minute. That difference offers a strong temptation to listeners to take mental excursions.[2]

What spoke to me in the opening words of this chapter was that it is not only important to listen well; we must also be aware of mental excursions. I believe it is very hard to separate mental fog and mental excursions. Even as I am writing this chapter and trying to stay focused, I can hear my wife listening to the weather channel in a nearby room.

I have only been to one PGA professional tournament. I can only imagine how hard it must be to stay focused on your game plan when you are one stroke ahead of your competitor two holes behind you. Suddenly you hear the crowd roar and the fog can start rolling in. The mind can start taking you in the wrong direction. Regaining your thoughts or getting back in focus certainly requires a conscientious decision that drives you away from the distraction and back to mental control.

As Christians who are trying to follow Christ scripturally, we must realize the power of the mind to distract and damage our walk with the Lord. Through my years of trying to serve the Lord, I have found many times that bad, negative, and unpleasant thoughts have driven me to God's word. Firstly, it drives me to what 1 John 1:8–10 says.

If we say we have no sin, we deceive ourselves, and the truth is not in us. If we confess our sins, he is faithful and just to forgive us our sins, and to cleanse us from all unrighteousness. If we say that we have not sinned, we make him a liar, and his word is not in us.

Our willingness to confess our sin does not resave us. It simply is agreeing with God that we still have this sin nature that we deal with. Confessing this sin keeps us walking in the light of Christ.

Secondly, it drives me to Philippians 4:4–8, which says,

Rejoice in the Lord always: and again I say, Rejoice. Let your moderation be known unto all men. The Lord is at hand. Be careful for nothing; but in every thing by prayer and supplication with thanks- giving let your requests be made known unto God. And the peace of God, which passeth all understanding, shall keep your hearts and minds through Christ Jesus. Finally, brethren, whatsoever things are true, whatsoever things are honest, whatsoever things are just, whatsoever things are pure, whatsoever things are lovely, whatsoever things are of good report; if there be any virtue, if there be any praise, think on these things.

In order to maintain these Christian virtues, rejoicing in the Lord, gentleness, and praying with thanksgiving, one needs to center the mind on certain things. Verse 8 gives some good options to think on.

Bottom line golf is a thinking game. Staying mentally alert is a plus in this game. Putting a lot of thought into all the different components of the game can determine success. Likewise, there are many components to life that one needs to think about. The Bible itself not only shows these components, but if one is willing to read, study and believe, it will also keep you spiritually alert while pointing you to a very present help.

God is our refuge and strength,
a very present help in trouble.
—Psalm 46:1

CHAPTER 18

Hazards

One of the ways my Webster dictionary defines *hazard* is "an obstacle, like a sand trap on a golf course." Three years ago, my wife and I played eighteen holes of golf at Pipestem State Park in West Virginia. As I was getting ready to hit one of my approach shots to the green on the front nine, we saw three wild turkeys scratching away in the sand trap. They were certainly enjoying this hazard a lot more than I enjoy them. The worst thing about golf is that one hazard or obstacle can seem to cause even the best golfer to end up in another one. I suppose one of the most dreaded hazards is water. The visibility of water can seem to get into the mind of the golfer and sometimes the outcome is not pretty. There certainly are a lot of obstacles to deal with in golf. This is another reason this game is so challenging and enjoyable. As you face them, it is essential to give some thought to them and have a good game plan. We all would have to agree that hazards do not just go away after the eighteenth hole.

There is also many hazards and obstacles in life. These, like the ones on the golf course, can lead to greater difficulties. I believe that God has put in place a good plan to make us aware of these and help us to avoid them. One of God's first plans is centered around a male and female that was created in his own image. Genesis 1:27–28 says,

> So God created man in his own image, in the image of God created he him; male and female created he them. And God blessed them, and God said unto them, Be fruitful, and multiply, and replenish the earth, and subdue it: and have dominion over the fish of the sea, and over the fowl of the air, and over every living thing that moveth upon the earth.

This is the beginning of a family plan. The first family started here.

Parental instruction was so needed then and is so needed today, to avoid the pitfalls in life that can only lead to greater problems. Paul, in Ephesians 6:1–4, not only gives some good parental instructions but also some good children instruction. He says,

> Children, obey your parents in the Lord: for this is right. Honour thy father and mother; which is the first commandment with promise; That it may be well with thee, and thou mayest live long on the earth. And, ye fathers, provoke not

your children to wrath: but bring them up in the nurture and admonition of the Lord.

The children need to obey and honor, while the father should not put unreasonable demands upon them or overcorrect them but should take the responsibility to teach and instruct them in the ways of the Lord. Parental instruction should be by word and example.

As bad as hazards are on the golf course, they become very small when it comes to the game of life. The same way the scorecard shows the hazard you face, the Bible shows many hazards and obstacles, but it also shows some good ways to overcome them.

And these words, which I command thee
this day, shall be in thine heart;
And thou shalt teach them diligently unto
thy children, and shalt talk of them
when thou sittest in thine house,
and when thou walkest by the way,
and when thou liest down, and when thou risest up.
And thou shalt bind them for a
sign upon thine hand,
and they shall be as frontlets between thine eyes.
And thou shalt write them upon
the posts of thy house,
and on thy gates.
—Deuteronomy 6:6–9

CHAPTER 19

Winning in the End

I suppose most of us have seen the little boy on television throwing up the ball and trying to hit it. All the while, he is saying, "I am the greatest hitter in the world." After missing the ball three times, he suddenly proclaims, "I am the greatest pitcher in the world."

Winning is very important in life. It seems to be a natural instinct in us and we all want to stand in the winner's circle. I am so glad we can, by way of the golf channels and other sports networks. Thanks to them, we can share a little of that winning feeling when we see those men and women receiving their trophies.

The winning desire, if not controlled in a proper way, can be very detrimental to us as well as to others. Cheating is one example, as well as gambling away money that could be used to help others. Bottom line is as good as it feels to win, feelings seem to wane or fade away as time unfolds. As I grow older and know time is running out, this becomes more of a reality.

Some things do not seem as important as they used to be and that is good.

My mother, Mildred Yoak, who lived to be ninety years old, used to talk to me as her pastor and son about dying and how she would handle it. I would always say that I could not answer that question, but would assure her that the Bible teaches that God's grace is sufficient. Her faith in Christ was very strong and she loved to talk about spiritual issues, as well as many other things. When she took her last breath at St. Joseph Hospital on March 1, 2009, I can humbly and thankfully say that she was a winner in the end. My brother, Bob, and I were there with her that Sunday evening and I will never forget what he said. He said, "Mom didn't go to church today. She went to heaven."

I honestly believe that scriptural faith is so needed in this game of life. Romans 10:17 says, "So then faith cometh by hearing, and hearing by the word of God." Hearing God's word and having faith in its message is a win-win situation. Scriptural faith can certainly be awakened in those who are willing to hear. This can lead to a life where one can walk by faith and not just by sight when faith comes into play. This becomes a winning combination.

Winning is very important in life, and it gets a lot of attention. Likewise, knowing and believing that within the written word of God there is a plan that can make you a winner in the end.

But whoso looketh into the perfect law of liberty,
and continueth therein, he being
not a forgetful hearer,
but a doer of the work, this man
shall be blessed in his deed.
—James 1:25

CHAPTER 20

Learning While Losing

I thoroughly enjoy watching the PGA and LPGA tournaments. I especially enjoy the fourth day when you get to hear the winner's response and sometimes even the losers'. Most of the time, we seem to associate the word *losing* with something bad, when in reality it can sometimes be good. Loss is such a part of life and no one is exempt from it. Losing is certainly something we have to keep in perspective, whether it is in golf or in life.

While writing this book, my wife and I have been attending some high school basketball games. Toward the end of one of them, a boy on the losing team fouled out. When he came and sat down, he started crying and we felt sorry for him. Loss, within the moment, is very hard and a very competitive spirit can make it worse. The good news is time erases those feelings and life continues on.

Everyone that reads the Bible has heard the phrase "a thorn in the flesh." Paul, the one that wrote so many of the books in the New Testament, experienced a thorn in the flesh. In 2 Corinthians 12:7–10, Paul relates this experience. He says,

> Lest I should be exalted above measure through the abundance of the revelations, there was given to me a thorn in the flesh, the messenger of Satan to buffet me, lest I should be exalted above measure. For this thing I besought the Lord thrice, that it might depart from me. And he said unto me, My grace is sufficient for thee: for my strength is made perfect in weakness. Most gladly therefore will I rather glory in my infirmities, that the power of Christ may rest upon me. Therefore I take pleasure in infirmities, in reproaches, in necessities, in persecutions, in distresses for Christ's sake: for when I am weak, then am I strong.

What I have always received from these words is that weaknesses can give opportunities for the power of the Lord to reside and be exhibited in our lives.

Divine power can be developed in human weakness. Weaknesses can drive us to something better if we choose to allow that. Even loss, when viewed in the right way, can be beneficial personally, as well as a tool to help and comfort others. Troubles and problems in life can sometimes make us feel like we are fighting a losing battle and that we are fighting alone.

The Bible teaches us that God is the Father of mercies and the God of all comfort who is able to comfort in a time of tribulation. Second Corinthians 1:3–4 says,

> Blessed be God, even the Father of our Lord Jesus Christ, the Father of mercies, and the God of all comfort; Who comforteth us in all our tribulation, that we may be able to comfort them which are in any trouble, by the comfort wherewith we ourselves are comforted of God.

Tribulation, which may involve loss, does not go unnoticed by the Lord. It can give one the opportunity to comfort others. Paul, who wrote these words and experienced God's comfort, knew this would enable him to become an extension of God's comfort. God does not comfort us so we can be comfortable but so we can comfort others.

When life comes at us hard, God's word can give us a different perspective on the hardships we may be dealing with. It can teach us during tribulation and help us to learn during losses.

> It is good for me that I have been afflicted;
> that I might learn thy statutes.
> —Psalm 119:71

CHAPTER 21

Encouragement

An encourager makes for a better environment on or off the golf course. It is always good to hear someone say, "Nice shot." I believe it is safe to say that there is an inward and an outward source of encouragement. A good frame of mind, whether one is playing golf or doing the many other requirements of life, can be an inward source of encouragement. The right attitude can take something that is bad and use it to spur one on to do better or try harder. The right frame of mind and a positive attitude not only encourage in a personal way but also are rewarding.

Emotions can get the best of us on or off the golf course. Being aware of this makes golf or whatever we are doing a more enjoyable experience. We all can be an inward source of encouragement if we set our heads to do so. Likewise, we all need to be an outward source of encouragement. Have you ever been around someone that makes you feel better about yourself than you did when you first started talking to them?

That person is an encourager, which is of great value. Honest encouragement, not flattery, is so needed today. Flattery tries to get something in return and is quite a contrast to honest encouragement.

Proverbs 26:28 says, "A lying tongue hateth those that are afflicted by it; and a flattering mouth worketh ruin." Lying and flattery seem to go hand in hand. Both are very destructive. Flattery can be an enemy to encouragement, as well as discouragement. Discouragement can have a proper place in life if it is used for the betterment of humanity. Bottom line is there certainly is a much-needed place in society today, for encouragement as well as discouragement.

The Bible gives good information on both of these. There is a man that we are introduced to in Acts 4 and he is characterized as an encourager. His name is Barnabas. Acts 4:36–37 says,

> And Joses, who by the apostles was surnamed Barnabas, (which is, being interpreted, The son of consolation,) a Levite, and of the country of Cyprus, Having land, sold it, and brought the money, and laid it at the apostles' feet.

This man certainly lived up to the name that the apostles gave him. He was not only a generous man but was also one that consoled and encouraged others while playing an important role in the early church.

A common theme for encouragement, as well as discouragement, is expressed in the New Testament by the word *exhort* or *exhortation*, which is translated sometimes as "encourage" or "encouragement." Other times, it carries the thought of warning or discouragement. Hebrews 10:24–25 says,

> And let us consider one another to provoke unto love and to good works: Not forsaking the assembling of ourselves together, as the manner of some is; but exhorting one another: and so much the more, as ye see the day approaching.

In these verses, you see an encouragement to consider one another and provoke unto love and good works. But you also see the writer trying to discourage, prevent, or warn them not to forsake the assembling of themselves together, especially since the second coming of Christ was drawing nearer.

I personally have been on the receiving end of encouragement many times in my years of ministry, and for that, I am grateful. I think it is good for us all to remember that so many things that cost nothing can mean so much.

As ye know how we exhorted and comforted
and charged every one of you, as a father
doth his children, That ye would walk worthy
of God, who hath called you unto his kingdom
and glory. For this cause also thank we God
without ceasing, because, when ye received the
word of God which ye heard of us, ye received it not
as the word of men, but as it is in
truth, the word of God,
which effectually worketh also in you that believe.
—1 Thessalonians 2:11–13

CHAPTER 22

Second Chances

We all like to play well and win in the golf world. I have always thought that golf is a game of second chances. If you do not play well on the front nine, there is always the back nine. On the courses my golfing buddies and I play, nothing seems to change except the pin placement once in a while. If you don't play well one week, you get another chance the next week.

I always enjoy playing golf at Mingo Bottom in Wirt County, West Virginia. They designate certain days that you can play all day with a cart for a certain price. They even give you two hot dogs and an iced tea for lunch. This is the perfect plan to experience a second chance. You can play eighteen holes and then get a second chance to improve on the next eighteen.

We live in a world where we all are probably recipients of second chances. If you realize this, it should raise the awareness of how important it is to give others a second chance. If you have ever studied the Bible, you will see this truth over and over. In my many years of walking this walk of faith, I have heard people say that God is a God of second chances. The Bible gives validity to this truth more than once. Jesus Christ verifies this in his words to the inhabitants of Jerusalem. He said in Luke 13:34–35,

> O Jerusalem, Jerusalem, which killest the prophets, and stonest them that are sent unto thee; how often would I have gathered thy children together as a hen doth gather her brood under her wings, and ye would not! Behold, your house is left unto you desolate: and verily I say unto you, Ye shall not see me, until the time come when ye shall say, Blessed is he that cometh in the name of the Lord.

There are four truths brought out here.

1. (He sent the prophets.) They ignored their message or killed them.
2. (How often.) More than once, he tried to reach them.
3. (Ye would not.) Refusal and rejection of God's word.
4. (Judgment.) They refused to change and failed to take advantage of the chances that the Lord gave them.

Ignoring second chances can be a recipe for disaster in the physical realm as well as the spiritual.

Very early in the book of Genesis, we see two brothers, Cain and Abel, sons of Adam and Eve, bringing offerings to the Lord. Genesis 4:3–8, says,

> And in process of time it came to pass, that Cain brought of the fruit of the ground an offering unto the Lord. And Abel, he also brought of the firstlings of his flock and the fat thereof. And the Lord had respect unto Abel and to his offering. But unto Cain and to his offering he had not respect. And Cain was very wroth, and his countenance fell. And the Lord said unto Cain, Why art thou wroth? And why is thy countenance fallen? If thou doest well, shalt thou not be accepted? And if thou doest not well, sin lieth at the door. And unto thee shall be his desire, and thou shalt rule over him. And Cain talked with Abel his brother: and it came to pass, when they were in the field, that Cain rose up against Abel his brother, and slew him.

Within these verses, we see the Lord rejecting or disapproving of Cain's offering, but we also see the Lord giving him a second chance to get it right. Yet Cain rejected the offer. The Lord tried to reason and rescue this man, but he failed to take advantage of it, which brought judgment upon himself and his civilization.

Appreciating second chances and taking advantage of them can be a pathway to blessings, both spiritually and physically.

> If my people, which are called by my name,
> shall humble themselves, and pray,
> and seek my face, and turn from their wicked ways;
> then will I hear from heaven, and will forgive
> their sin, and will heal their land.
> —2 Chronicles 7:14

CHAPTER 23

Dressing for Success

Another one of the enjoyments in the golf world is seeing all the different kinds of clothing worn by the various different golfers. Dress seems to be prominent in golf as well as lots of other professions. Dress not only gets the fans attention, but quite often, you hear the announcer making mention of it.

I suppose most of us have seen those signs that say, "No shoes, no shirt, no service." Proper dress seems to have invaded all facets of life. There seems to be clothing designed for whatever the occasion might be. There are certainly a lot of choices for the consumer. It is almost like trying to buy a toothbrush or toothpaste. It can be a challenge. Dress is very influential in our society today. Needless to say, dress has a voice. It says something both publicly and personally, whether we like it or not. I think it is safe to say that dress plays a role in success. Most people want to be successful in life. Many things factor into this equation of success: one's choices, priorities, abilities, opportunities, education, work ethic, appearance, and even dress. We seem to have somewhat control over most of these if we choose to, especially dress. Proper dress certainly faces problems from a world that wants to set a dress code that can be very persuasive and provocative. Bottom line is we all need something to counteract the culture we live in, especially if it is detrimental to one's success, physically as well as spiritually.

The word of God is a good option to turn to; it deals with the inward as well as the outward of humankind. Some words that the Lord spoke to Samuel, when he was told to go and anoint a new king of Israel, drive home this point. First Samuel 16:7 says, "But the Lord said unto Samuel, Look not on his countenance, or on the height of his stature; because I have refused him: for the Lord seeth not as man seeth; for man looketh on the outward appearance, but the Lord looketh on the heart." I believe this scripture shows God is more interested in the heart or inward part of humanity than the outward. I do not believe this verse is trying to undermine the importance of proper dress. After all, in Genesis 3, we see God coming to Adam and Eve after they had sinned in the Garden of Eden. At this time, they realized they were naked and attempted to cover themselves. This was inadequate, so God took the skins of animals and clothed them. From a scriptural point of view, dress goes farther than the outward. The Bible uses the analogy of putting on and putting off garments to enhance one morally as well as spiritually. Colossians 3:8–13 says,

> But now ye also put off all these; anger, wrath, malice, blasphemy, filthy communication out of your mouth. Lie not one to another, seeing that ye have put off the old man with his deeds; And have put on the new man, which is renewed in knowledge after the image of him that created him: Where there is neither Greek nor Jew, circumcision nor uncircumcision, Barbarian, Scythian, bond nor free: but Christ is all and in all. Put on therefore. As the elect of God, holy and beloved, bowels of mercies, kindness, humbleness of mind, meekness, longsuffering: Forbearing one another, and forgiving one another, if any man have a quarrel against any: even as Christ forgave you, so also do ye.

Paul, who wrote these words, knew the importance of putting on a spiritual wardrobe and the impact it could have on others.

In Romans 13:14, Paul says, "But put ye on the Lord Jesus Christ, and make not provision for the flesh, to fulfill its lusts." If the truths taught in these scriptures are a priority in one's life, it is not only a step in the right direction, but it also can be a starting point for dressing for success.

Put on the whole armour of God, that ye may
be able to stand against the wiles of the devil.
For we wrestle not against flesh and blood, but
against principalities, against powers,
against the rulers of the darkness of this world,
against spiritual wickedness in high places.
Wherefore take unto you the whole armour
of God, that ye may be able to withstand in the
evil day, and having done all, to stand. Stand
therefore, having your loins girt about with
truth, and having on the
breastplate of righteousness; And your feet
shod with the preparation of the gospel of peace;
Above all taking the shield of faith, wherewith
ye shall be able to quench all the fiery darts
of the wicked. And take the helmet of salvation,
and the sword of the Spirit, which is
the word of God.
—Ephesians 6:11–17

CHAPTER 24

The Right Equipment

Over the fifty plus years that I have played golf, it seems the right equipment to help us improve our game has evolved to a new level. The irons, drivers, putters, balls, grips, bags, carts, and even ball retrievers have all improved over the years. One year my wife got me a nice ball retriever for Christmas. She goes with me sometimes when I go to play by myself, so she realized I needed this extra piece of equipment. That present has been very helpful and has saved me some money but has not lowered my score. The right equipment to make one's golf experience memorable goes far beyond what we put in the golf bag. Am I really seeing golf shoes that have a dial on the back that somehow adjusts the cleats? How cool is that!

One has to marvel at the ingenuity and technology that we see, not only in our great country but worldwide today. It is incredible the wisdom that has been granted humankind to carry this out. Where this knowledge and wisdom have come from could be debatable.

Personally, I have to believe our Creator is behind it all. He has allowed man and woman, whom he created in His own image, to play a major role in making this planet Earth a place that would be inhabitable for all living things.

Genesis 1:26–28, says,

> And God said, Let us make man in our image, after our likeness: and let them have dominion over the fish of the sea, and over the fowl of the air, and over the cattle, and over all the earth, and over every creeping thing that creepeth upon the earth. So God created man in his own image, in the image of God created he him; male and female created he them. And God blessed them, and God said unto them, Be fruitful, and multiply, and replenish the earth, and subdue it: and have dominion over the fish of the sea, and over the fowl of the air, and over every living thing that moveth upon the earth.

If one is to read this with an open mind and believe it, you see very early here in the book of Genesis how God has given humankind a stewardship role. Humankind was to take care of creation or to have dominion over it. Within this first mandate, given to the male and female, we see a call for them to be fruitful, multiply, replenish the earth, and subdue it. The word *subdue* in the Hebrew language means to "tread down, conquer, or to bring into subjection." Many Bible scholars believe this mandate or commission to subdue or conquer embraces all human activity, such as science, technology, research, study, and developments in the medical field, plus all the other various advancements we see in civilization.

I so enjoy watching some of the programs on television that show how all the different things that we use, need, and enjoy are made. Seeing all of these achievements firsthand should raise the question of why this is all happening and where this wisdom came from to achieve all of it. I believe that humankind is carrying out a mandate for God and many who are doing it may not even believe in Him.

A careful study of God's word reveals that He uses all humanity to carry out His plan and His purpose. I feel through all the research, technology, achievements, and ingenuity that seems to have come from the hands of man is accomplished because of an unseen hand.

How thankful we should all be for the technology and the right equipment that so greatly improves our lives. The knowledge that has been granted to humankind to accomplish all of this ought to cause us all to say, "Give God the glory, all ye people."

Oh that men would praise the Lord for his goodness,
and for his wonderful works to the children of men!
For he satisfieth the longing soul,
and filleth the hungry soul with goodness.
—Psalm 107:8–9

CHAPTER 25

A Good Follow-through

This is a term I have always heard in reference to golf. I have to remind myself of the importance of this sometimes as I play. It seems so easy to get out of sync in fundamental things in golf. I heard it said one time that a house does not suddenly deteriorate or a garden does not suddenly become overgrown with weeds. It happens in a very subtle way. Paying attention and trying to stay on top of our game and the game of life is so important. I suppose the term "a good follow-through" is not only good to consider in golf but in life itself. Life is made up of many different parts. Time has a way of robbing us of what is important. Time can run out and the opportunity to follow through is gone.

We all have used or heard the phrase "When I get around to it." It is very familiar and almost humorous but can be very costly in the physical as well as the spiritual realm. Proverbs 27:1 says, "Boast not thyself of tomorrow; for thou knowest not what a day may bring forth." We all can certainly be presumptuous or assume that we have plenty of time to address an issue or get it done.

The word of God reminds us again and again of the uncertainty of time and how dangerous it is to delay or put things off. A good example of this is seen in a parable Jesus spoke in Luke 12:16–21,

> And he spake a parable unto them, saying, The ground of a certain rich man brought forth plentifully: And he thought within himself, saying, What shall I do, because I have no room where to bestow my fruits? And he said, This will I do: I will pull down my barns, and build greater; and there will I bestow all my fruits and my goods. And I will say to my soul, Soul, thou hast much goods laid up for many years; take thine ease, eat, drink, and be merry. But God said unto him, Thou fool, this night thy soul shall be required of thee: then whose shall those things be, which thou hast provided? So is he that layeth up treasure for himself, and is not rich toward God.

Here was a man that made at least four bad assumptions.

1. He assumed that he could depend on his own reasoning or thoughts. Proverbs 3:5–6 says, "Trust in the Lord with all thine heart; and lean

not unto thine own understanding. In all thy ways acknowledge him, and he shall direct thy paths."

2. He assumed that "I" was the most important.
3. He assumed "things" would satisfy and bring happiness.
4. He assumed he was taking care of his future.

This parable paints a picture of a man who was rich materialistically but poor spiritually. God refers to this man as a fool. This fool's walk was shown by his words; the Lord was not in the picture until he died. Making assumptions, when the Lord is not in the picture leads to bad endings.

James 4:13–15 gives some good advice about inviting the Lord into your plans. James says,

> Go to now, ye that say, Today or tomorrow we will go into such a city, and continue there a year, and buy and sell, and get gain: Whereas ye know not what shall be on the morrow. For what is your life? It is even a vapour, that appeareth for a little time and then vanisheth away. For that ye ought to say, If the Lord will, we shall live, and do this or that.

In light of how brief and uncertain life is, we need to include the Lord in our plans. If he is in our heart, he ought to be in our speech. We should never be ashamed to say if it is the Lord's will.

The value of a good follow-through can go far beyond the golf course. Failing to follow through on things we know we should do or be doing can be costly to us as well as others.

> For I am now ready to be offered, and the time
> of my departure is at hand. I have fought a good
> fight, I have finished my course, I have kept the
> faith: Henceforth there is laid up for me a crown
> of righteousness, which the Lord, the righteous
> judge, shall give me at that day: and not to me only,
> but unto all them also that love his appearing.
> —2 Timothy 4:6–8

CHAPTER 26

Fore

A loud fore on the golf course sure gets my attention. I always try to take cover or at least cover my head with my hands. By the time you hear this verbal alert, I am of the mind that it is too late to do a whole lot about it. This vocal alarm system, along with hand and arm gestures of which way the ball is heading, seems to be the best warning system for those who might be in the flight path of the ball. Of all my years of watching golf, it seems to be a rare occurrence for someone to be hit with a golf ball. This speaks very loudly of how accurate the men and women are who play on the professional level.

In this modern age that we are living in, there seems to be an abundance of warning systems. Some of these systems are vocal while others are visible. The vehicles we are blessed to have today seem to have symbols, chimes, or reminders to keep us safe as well as prevent costly repairs. Failure to pay attention to or utilize these things can lead to a bad ending.

My mother, Mildred Yoak, sister Patricia Nedeff, my wife, and I had the privilege of visiting Mount St. Helens in 1989, a few years after it erupted. It was a visible reminder of the power and devastation of the volcano that occurred there. It also was a reminder of some that did not pay attention to the verbal warnings to leave that area, especially those living around the lake at the base of the mountain.

We all have access to the written word of God. There are many verbal warnings throughout its pages that are designed to help one live a good life and die a good death. The Lord used humankind as a voice to help us see ourselves as well as see the Lord. Moses, who was a voice for the Lord, led the children of Israel out of the bondage of the Egyptians and prepared them to enter the Promised Land. In this preparation, Moses was asking God's people to remember some things. Deuteronomy 8:1–2,10–14, says,

> All the commandments which I command thee this day shall ye observe to do, that ye may live, and multiply, and go in and possess the land which the Lord sware unto your fathers. And thou shalt remember all the way which the Lord thy God led thee these forty years in the wilderness, to humble thee, and to prove thee, to know what was in thine heart, whether thou wouldest keep his commandments, or no ... When thou hast eaten and art full, then thou

shalt bless the Lord thy God for the good land which he hath given thee. Beware that thou forget not the Lord thy God, in not keeping his commandments, and his judgments, and his statures, which I command thee this day: Lest when thou hast eaten and art full, and hast built goodly houses, and dwelt therein; And when thy herds and flocks multiply, and thy silver and thy gold is multiplied, and all that thou hast is multiplied; Then thine heart be lifted up, and thou forget the Lord thy God, which brought thee forth out of the land of Egypt, from the house of bondage.

Moses is not only reminding them of God's commandments, but he is also warning them about forgetting after they enter the land that is flowing with milk and honey. Moses was like a vocal alarm system that was warning this new generation of Israelites who would soon be possessing this new land.

Today, the New Testament believer can learn so much from the Old Testament. In Romans 15:4, Paul says, "For whatsoever things were written aforetime were written for our learning, that we through patience and comfort of the scriptures might have hope." The Old Testament is not only to help us learn, but it also promotes patience, brings comfort, and enhances hope. The God of the Old Testament came to humankind in the New Testament as the Lord Jesus Christ, who is the Savior of the world. The words of Jesus and His warnings have changed the lives of millions of people who have put their faith and trust in Him for the free gift of salvation that is offered to whosoever will. Romans 10:13 says, "For whosoever shall call upon the name of the Lord shall be saved."

Fore is just a little four-letter word that is designed to alert one of danger. Faith is only a five-letter word, and the middle letter is *i*. Faith in the Lord Jesus Christ not only saves us but it also can make us appreciate the words and the warnings of the greatest book ever written.

Wherewithal shall a young man cleanse his way?
By taking heed thereto according to thy word.
With my whole heart have I sought thee:
O let me not wander from thy commandments.
Thy word have I hid in mine heart,
that I might not sin against thee.
—Psalm 119:9–11

CHAPTER 27

Keeping Score

Keeping score is an important part of golf. It requires honesty and accuracy. When I play in a foursome, we usually ask one person to keep score. Some of the players will keep their own score also. This allows us to keep tabs on how well our playing partners are doing and helps us watch our own numbers.

I was tired of the winter weather here in West Virginia and itching to play some golf. My wife and I decided to go to Myrtle Beach for a week. While we were there, I played some golf. My wife rode along with me and kept score for me. After playing eighteen holes, I was looking at the scorecard and noticed how detailed she was in keeping my score. She had even wrote down every time I hit a tree. I told her she did not have to give out all that information. Talk about honesty and accuracy!

Keeping score is not only about honesty and accuracy. It is about keeping tally numerically, and this goes far beyond the golf course. The small numbers in golf is important, while the big numbers in so many of life's activities seems more important. The more things we have, the better off we presume to be. If one fails to keep tally numerically, things can become a burden and not a blessing. I read a quote several years ago and do not know who spoke the words. It said, "Get all you can, from whoever you can, however you can, as often as you can, and can all you get then sit on the can." May I say, with kindness in my heart, trying to fill all the cans in life can be costly, if that is what your life is focused on.

The Bible is a book that asks us to take tally of what is happening in our life and shows us how to have balance in our life. In Paul's closing words in 2 Corinthians 13:5, he says, "Examine yourselves, whether ye be in the faith; prove your own selves. Know ye not your own selves, how that Jesus Christ is in you, except ye be reprobates?" It is easy to examine others, but here Paul asks his readers to test themselves to see if their faith is in Jesus Christ. Christ said in Matthew 16:24–26,

> Then said Jesus unto his disciples, If any man will come after me, let him deny himself, and take up his cross, and follow me. For whosoever will save his life shall lose it: and whosoever will lose his life for my sake shall find it. For what is a man profited, if he shall gain the whole world, and lose his own soul? Or what shall a man give in exchange for his soul?

Life is so much more than self and so much more than gain. It is so foolish to try to possess all the things of the world at the expense of losing one's soul.

A careful study of God's word shows that the soul is in the hands of God and is destined for salvation or damnation. If one is willing to believe these truths from God's word and act upon them, by faith, it can make the game of life more meaningful. Keeping tally on the golf course is important, but even more important is keeping tabs in life.

Lay not up for yourselves treasures upon earth,
where moth and rust doth corrupt, and where
thieves break through and steal: But lay up
for yourselves treasures in heaven,
where neither moth nor rust doth corrupt,
and where thieves do not break through nor steal.
For where your treasure is, there will
your heart be also.
—Matthew 6:19–21

CHAPTER 28

Penalty Strokes

Penalty strokes in the game of golf can play a major role in the success of the game. Regardless of how good of a player one is, these penalties can rear up their ugly head on about any hole. The humility of a penalty stroke really seems to intensify, especially if you are a repeat offender on the same hole. I think it is safe to say a penalty is a form of punishment. Best-case scenario, punishment should correct or teach a lesson. I suppose the next time I have two penalty strokes on a hole I should stop mumbling and complaining and think about what I learned from this.

I play golf periodically at the St. Marys Golf Club in Pleasants County, West Virginia. This golf course is located next to the St. Marys Correctional Center. Every time I play there, my mind always goes to those that are incarcerated in that place. The penalties or punishment we receive on a golf course is very minimal compared to those that have lost their freedom. I helped do a church service a few years ago in that prison.

It was an eerie feeling going in there, but my first impression was that these men were just ordinary-looking people who had stepped out of bounds in relationship to the law and were paying the penalty for it. During the church service, it was a blessing to see some of the men being not only involved in the service but also responding to the message of God's word. I really believe if many of these men would have responded to the message and teaching of the word of God earlier, they might not have had to deal with this chapter in their lives.

The consequences that result from bad decisions can be very hurtful to us and to others. The penalty for our actions can be paid, but the memory is hard to erase. The Bible teaches a principle in Galatians 6:6–9, that one needs to think long and hard when we are tempted to do something that we know is wrong. It says,

> Let him that is taught in the word communicate unto him that teaches in all good things. Be not deceived; God is not mocked: for whatsoever a man soweth, that shall he also reap. For he that soweth to his flesh shall of the flesh reap corruption; but he that soweth to the Spirit shall of the Spirit reap life everlasting. And let us not be weary in well doing: for in due season we shall reap, if we faint not.

Paul uses sowing and reaping, something the culture of that day would be very familiar with, to teach an important spiritual principle. If one only sows to the flesh/human nature, one will reap corruption, something that ruins or decays. On the other hand, sowing to the spirit results in spiritual treasure plus reaping life everlasting. There is a privilege in these verses as well as a promise. We can do what we choose to do, but we can be assured that repercussions from our actions may follow us the rest of our lives. I feel the best thing to strive for is to not give up trying to do what is right.

A penalty stroke or a bad decision on the golf course is temporal, especially if we par or birdie the next hole. On and off the golf course, we all need some help when it comes to choices. God's word is a good option that is full of truths that promote good choices that lead to fewer penalty strokes in life.

By faith Moses, when he was come to years,
refused to be called the son of Pharaoh's daughter;
Choosing rather to suffer affliction
with the people of God,
than to enjoy the pleasures of sin for a season;
Esteeming the reproach of Christ greater riches
than the treasures in Egypt: for he had respect
unto the recompence of the reward.
—Hebrews 11:24–26

CHAPTER 29

Watching

Golf certainly has a watching element about it. Fact of the matter is if you are playing in a foursome, you probably do more watching on the golf course than actually playing. One of my favorite ways of relaxing at home is watching golf. It takes me places I will never get to go, plus I get to see things I would never get to see. I enjoy watching great golf shots, all the beautiful scenery, and any wildlife that is around the golf course. Hats off to all the great camera crews for adding another dimension to the game of golf.

We live in a world that allows us to see more than we need to see sometimes. The phrase "That is not fit to watch" has taken on another meaning as technology has advanced and morals have declined.

Several years ago, I sang in the choir at Vaught Chapel Church in Leachtown, West Virginia. Doris George was the choir director and she taught us the song titled "You Are the Only Bible Some People Read." This song rings out a message, loud and clear, that our life is being watched. Throughout my many years of preaching and ministering to others, I have made reference to just how important the title of this song is to me and to others. If one really values the message of the Bible, it behooves us not to discredit it by bad behavior. It is a book that fosters morals. What we choose to do and watch says a lot about our moral condition.

Psalm 101:1–4 says,

> I will sing of mercy and judgment: unto thee, O Lord, will I sing. I will behave myself wisely in a perfect way. O when wilt thou come unto me? I will walk within my house with a perfect heart. I will set no wicked thing before mine eyes: I hate the work of them that turn aside; it shall not cleave to me. A froward heart shall depart from me: I will not know a wicked person.

The psalmist David saw God as being merciful and just. This would motivate him to live wisely and to cultivate wise behavior. This wise behavior would be developed by his eyes, heart, and associations.

From a scriptural point of view, watching goes beyond the physical in relationship to the second coming of Jesus Christ. The Bible tells us to watch in Matthew 24:36–42,

But of that day and hour knoweth no man, no, not the angels of heaven, but my Father only. But as the days of Noah were, so shall also the coming of the Son of man be. For as in the days that were before the flood they were eating and drinking, marrying and giving in marriage, until the day that Noah entered into the ark, And knew not until the flood came, and took them all away; so shall also the coming of the Son of man be. Then shall two be in the field; the one shall be taken, and the other left. Two women shall be grinding at the mill; the one shall be taken, and the other left. Watch therefore: for ye know not what hour your Lord doth come.

When I read this, it appears that people in Noah's day were just going about living their lives, unconcerned about their spiritual welfare, when God suddenly brought judgment upon them by a worldwide flood.

A careful study of Genesis 6–8 shows why God brought this judgment and only spared Noah and his family. The people of that day apparently did not think anything was going to happen. The same mind-set will be characterized by the majority of people in relationship to the second coming of Christ. The warning is clear: everyone needs to watch or be vigilant or alert because no one knows the time this will happen. If our focus is only on the present, we are living an empty life. Things can be taken away from us very suddenly and unexpectedly. Temporal things, whether they seem good or bad, can only last so long.

If we study the Bible and believe the truths that it is teaching, it will help develop an eternal perspective. This can help us discern and see things for what they are and appreciate things that we cannot see. Spiritual vision adds another dimension to life.

> While we look not at the things which are seen,
> but at the things which are not seen:
> for the things which are seen are temporal;
> but the things which are not seen are eternal.
> —2 Corinthians 4:18

CHAPTER 30

Giving Back

Golf seems to be a sport that gives back so much. You hardly ever watch a golf event in which you do not hear the announcers talking about this topic. It is very heart warming when you hear of this spirit of generosity in the golf world. It would be unfair for me to say that golf is the only sport that shows this quality. I am sure this happens in other parts of the sports world. Think of how much golf gives to us that loves the game, whether you are a professional or amateur. As I am writing this chapter, I am planning to play a round this afternoon. This will not only give me some time to spend with my wife but will also give me an opportunity to work on my game before I start playing weekly with my golfing buddies.

Giving is such an important part of life. I think it is safe to say it is not something we are born with. It is a learned behavior that needs to be taught by word and example. This quality seems to be shown easier by some than others. Most have heard the phrase "That person would give you the shirt off their back." In doing many funerals and memorial services over the years, I have heard from many family members concerning their departed loved one that he or she was a giving person. What a good legacy or memory to leave.

I suppose if there is a common theme in the Bible it would be giving. Giving is certainly a two-way street. First, God is portrayed as a divine giver. Everyone, whether we want to acknowledge it or not, is a recipient of this giving God. Jesus drives home this point in the great Sermon on the Mount, when he is teaching about how we should respond to those that may not like us. In Matthew 5:43–45, he says,

> Ye have heard that it hath been said, Thou shalt love thy neighbour, and hate thine enemy. But I say unto you, Love your enemies, bless them that curse you, do good to them that hate you, and pray for them which despitefully use you, and persecute you; That ye may be the children of your Father which is in heaven: for he maketh his sun to rise on the evil and on the good, and sendeth rain on the just and on the unjust.

The point is the divine giver does not discriminate in giving. He sends the sun to shine on the evil and the good as well as the rain on the just and unjust. Jesus asks us to give our love to those that do not seem to deserve it. James, who is most likely the half brother of Jesus, had a good handle on this divine giver that does not discriminate. It says in James 1:17, "Every good gift and every perfect gift is from above, and cometh down from the Father of lights, with whom is no variableness, neither shadow of turning." James saw nothing but good coming from God, who he designates as the Father of lights that does not change.

So many of the good gifts in life come from above. God is the supreme example of giving, which is shown in His great plan of salvation or rescue for humankind. The greatest act of giving was when He came to this earth in the person of His Son and was willing to go to a cross and shed His blood for us. He paid a debt He did not owe because we owed a debt we could not pay. We all benefit so much from a giving Creator and so many others can benefit, if we have a giving spirit. Paul gives some good personal advice when it comes to giving. Second Corinthians 9:6–8 says,

> But this I say, He which soweth sparingly shall reap also sparingly; and he which soweth bountifully shall reap also bountifully. Every man according as he purposeth in his heart, so let him give; not grudgingly, or of necessity: for God loveth a cheerful giver. And God is able to make all grace abound toward you; that ye, always having all sufficiency in all things, may abound to every good work.

Paul uses a sowing example to illustrate the rewards of generous giving. One needs to make the choice in one's heart, but the results are very clear. Your cheerful giving allows God's grace to abound toward you both spiritually and physically. Giving that is done in the right spirit, regardless of the size, brings blessings to the giver and the receiver. Paul's parting words to the Christians at Ephesus in Acts 20:35 teaches a truth worth remembering. He said, "I have shewed you all things, how that so labouring ye ought to support the weak, and to remember the words of the Lord Jesus, how he said, It is more blessed to give than to receive." The blessings of giving outweighs the blessings of receiving.

I for one am thankful for a game that gives so much back, in a physical way as well as an enjoyable way. But most of all, I am thankful for the Lord who supplies all of our needs according to His riches in glory by Christ Jesus.

Give, and it shall be given unto you; good measure,
pressed down, and shaken
together, and running over,
shall men give into your bosom.
For with the same measure that
ye mete withal it shall be
measured to you again.
—Luke 6:38

CHAPTER 31

Talking to the Ball

It is almost humorous when you stop and think about verbally communicating to a golf ball. If you have played this game much, it is probably safe to say you have done this at one time or another. It certainly makes you feel good when the ball listens. In my case, it seems the ball is always hard of hearing and goes where it wants to anyway. Talking, whether it comes from those participating in or watching, seems to be another element to the game of golf. As you watch golf, you can count on hearing some verbal outburst from a dominant voice in the gallery that explodes, "Get in the hole!" Unlike other sports the talk stops, at least most of the time, while the player is hitting the shot. Microphones, placed throughout the golf course in professional events, allow those watching to hear some of the golf course talk. It is very commendable to say that almost all you hear from these golfers is family friendly.

Language says so much about all of us. In this day of modern technology, we can hear and see so much. In the advertising world, it is entertaining and amusing to see and hear all the animation and voices that are given to various things to sell the product. Who would have ever thought a few years ago that we would one day have a car that can tell us how to get to our destination? My son, Gary, who is legally blind, has a computer, alarm clock, and wristwatch that talk to him. Mechanical communication is a controlled form of talk, whereas human communication, at best, falls short of being controlled so many times. Talk has a good side as well as a bad side. Words can convince, as well as caution. They can complain as well as comfort. They can insult as well as instruct and help as well as hurt. We have all heard the phrase "Sticks and stones may break my bones, but words will never hurt me." To believe the last part of this is not being in the real world. Most of us have probably said things, at one time or another that we wish we had not said.

An unbridled tongue can cause great damage. The Bible addresses this issue in James 3:2–5.

> For in many things we offend all. If any man offend not in word, the same is a perfect man, and able also to bridle the whole body. Behold, we put bits in the horses' mouths, that they may obey us; and we turn about their whole body. Behold also the ships, which though they be great, and

are driven of fierce winds, yet are they turned about with a very small helm, whithersoever the governor listeth. Even so the tongue is a little member, and boasteth great things. Behold, how great a matter a little fire kindleth!

Within these verses, we see something small that can offend, direct, and destroy if it is not controlled. Earlier in James's writings, he gives some good advice that can help all of us if taken to heart. James 1:19 says, "Wherefore, my beloved brethren, let every man be swift to hear, slow to speak, slow to wrath." Beside this verse in my Bible, I have written, "There are two kinds of speakers: those who have something to say and those who have to say something."

I suppose we golfers, as long as we are able to play, will continue to say something to the golf ball. Honestly, we all know as powerful as words are, they are not going to affect what the golf ball does or where it ends up. On the other hand, I think it is safe to say our spoken words not only affect us but others also. Words make such a difference, but when it comes to talking to a golf ball, it is still very questionable.

Let no corrupt communication proceed out
of your mouth, but that which is good to the
use of edifying, that it may minister
grace unto the hearers.
—Ephesians 4:29

CHAPTER 32

The Lost Ball

Gary Conger, one of my golfing buddies, suggested that I write a chapter on the lost ball. I guess he thought we were experienced in that field. So here goes! I suppose this is an appropriate place for this chapter, since I just finished writing about talking to the ball. Talk certainly intensifies when you lose a ball. Losing a golf ball is bad enough, plus you lose a stroke and it might even cause you to lose the game. I guess it softens the blow if you find another ball better than yours, while you are looking for the one you lost.

Several years ago, I used to play golf with Bud Hays, a gentleman and good Christian man who attended the church I pastored in Vienna, West Virginia. We were playing golf at South Hills in Parkersburg. I believe it was the ninth hole on the front nine of the course. The first or second shot, depending on how well you hit the ball, had to cross a small stream of water that had some huge rocks on the one side. One of our shots, or maybe both of them, ended up in the hazard. While Bud and I were looking for our balls, I got down on my knees to look into a small opening under one of the large rocks. To my surprise, there were golf balls lying everywhere in a large opening underneath this rock. Needless to say, those lost balls turned into us finding about fifteen other balls. I guess the moral of this story is that loss is not always bad. For years, Bud and I talked and laughed about the discovery of that day.

When one stops to think about it, joy can come from loss. As a boy, I grew up in rural Calhoun County, West Virginia. The boys in that day were always trying to work to earn some money. My father, Lloyd Yoak, always taught my brother, Bob, and me to work. It was not always pleasant at the time, but I look back on that chapter of my life and I am thankful that our dad taught us a good work ethic. When I was not working at home, I would work for someone else to get some extra money. I used to work in the hay fields for a neighbor who had a farm. His name was Emanuel Hersman, and his son Larry was my best friend. We worked many hours together on his father's farm. I remember one day, while helping put up hay in one of the fields, I lost my billfold. I searched that hay field over and over, finally finding my billfold that had ten dollars in it. Needless to say, there was joy unspeakable that day.

More than once the Bible talks about how loss can result in joy. Jesus used parables to teach this truth. Luke 15:1–10, says,

> Then drew near unto him all the publicans and sinners for to hear him. And the Pharisees and scribes murmured, saying, This man receiveth sinners, and eateth with them. And he spake this parable unto them saying, What man of you, having an hundred sheep, if he lose one of them, doth not leave the ninety and nine in the wilderness, and go after that which is lost, until he find it? And when he hath found it, he layeth it on his shoulders, rejoicing. And when he cometh home, he calleth together his friends and neighbours, saying unto them, Rejoice with me; for I have found my sheep which was lost. I say unto you, that likewise joy shall be in heaven over one sinner that repenteth, more than over ninety and nine just persons which need no repentance. Either what woman having ten pieces of silver, if she lose one piece, doth not light a candle, and sweep the house, and seek diligently till she find it? And when she hath found it, she calleth her friends and her neighbours together, saying, Rejoice with me; for I have found the piece which I had lost. Likewise, I say unto you, there is joy in the presence of the angels of God over one sinner that repenteth.

Within these two parables, we see a man and a woman who had suffered loss. These parables drive home some important truths about loss. First, loss can get plenty of attention. Second, loss results in a search. Third, loss can result in joy. Jesus, in these parables, was attempting to show the Pharisees and Scribes the lack of concern they had for the spiritually lost, and he was trying to show his concern for them. When someone who is lost is found, it gets heaven's attention and that results in joy. For this to happen, the search must be diligent. This diligent search is very needed today, by all who have experienced the life that Jesus offers to those who choose to believe. The more one studies and tries to identify with the message and mission of God's word, the more this search should intensify.

Our physical losses, whether on the golf course or in life, can be very hurtful as well as helpful, if we allow it to guide us in the right direction.

> For the Son of man is come to seek
> and to save that which is lost.
> —Luke 19:10

CHAPTER 33

Quietness

Honestly, would you like to be one of those standing by the best golfers in the world while holding one of those signs asking everyone to be quiet? Most seem to obey this courtesy, other than the birds. The quietness on the golf course is another one of the good qualities about this game.

I remember my son, Gary, who is legally blind, talking about the importance of quietness. He learned this while taking mobility training in Charleston, West Virginia. One of his training sessions involved crossing busy streets in the city. Quietness was an indicator that the traffic had stopped and it was safe to cross.

If you have ever pulled up alongside one of those cars with the music—I suppose it was music—so loud that it vibrated your vehicle, it should give you a greater appreciation for quietness.

If you are an outdoorsman like me who has been in the woods many times before daybreak, it does not take long to see that quietness was built into God's creative design. I like to hunt turkey gobblers in the spring in Ritchie County, West Virginia. This hunt requires you to be in the woods at the break of day. As I would walk back into the woods before daylight, the only birds that I would hear were whippoorwills. When daylight started breaking, all the birds that make the woods their home would wake up singing. It was music to my ears, especially if the old gobbler chimed in.

As time unfolds, I suppose the quietness that we all need has suffered at the hands of progress. Quiet time is quality time since we live in a very noisy world. Even with all the ear protection that we have to drown out excessive noise, we still need to unclutter our lives and enjoy the quietness that our Creator intended for humankind. One of the most familiar psalms in the Bible echoes quietness. Psalm 23:1–3 says,

> The Lord is my shepherd; I shall not want. He maketh me to lie down in green pastures: he leadeth me beside the still waters. He restoreth my soul: he leadeth me in the paths of righteousness for his name's sake.

Lying down in the green pastures and being led by still waters certainly implies quietness. This is where the Lord can restore one's soul. There is a good side to quietness, but on the other hand, noise cannot only damage us physically but can hinder us spiritually.

In another one of the psalms, we see that God's desire is to be exalted in the earth. For this to happen, one must know God. Knowing God involves being still. Psalm 46:10 says, "Be still, and know that I am God: I will be exalted among the heathen, I will be exalted in the earth." Being away from noise and distractions can be such an important aspect to life.

The quietness of a golf course, when the only noise that you can hear is coming from nature, may be a rare thing. However, it can be a valuable thing not only to your game but also to the game of life.

And Moses said unto the people,
Fear ye not, stand still,
and see the salvation of the Lord,
which he will shew to you today:
for the Egyptians whom ye have seen today,
ye shall see them again no more for ever.
The Lord shall fight for you,
and ye shall hold your peace.
—Exodus 14:13–14

CHAPTER 34

The Senior Tour

It is most enjoyable to see all the golfers fifty years or older still playing, enjoying and competing on the Champions Tour.

Recently, I saw Jack Nicklaus, Lee Trevino, and Gary Player competing against some of the older golf greats. Don January, who was eighty-six years old, was in the mix. The announcer said at this age he could still hit the ball 270 yards. When I heard this, I could not help but to think of my friend Norvil Deem, who lived to be ninety-two years old. At the age of eighty-six he was still playing good golf and was always ready to be a part of our foursome. What a legacy all of the older men and women are leaving in the golf world. Age may mess up our swing pattern and limit our mobility, but it cannot take away the desire to play.

You cannot help but to wonder what would be in the record books if Sam Snead, Ben Hogan, Bobby Jones, and Bryon Nelson could have had the equipment that is available today. When you stop and think about it, they and all the older legends in golf played a major role in the development, technology, and advancing the game to the level we see today.

Age, as hard as it is, can make so many good contributions to life. The older generation has a lot of wisdom to pass on that is only experienced with age. Great value is put on age in the Bible. Paul, when he wrote to Titus, told him in Titus 2:1–5,

> But speak thou the things which become sound doctrine. That the aged men be sober, grave, temperate, sound in faith, in charity, in patience. The aged women likewise, that they be in behaviour as becometh holiness, not false accusers, not given to much wine, teachers of good things; That they may teach the young women to be sober, to love their husbands, to love their children, To be discreet, chaste, keepers at home, good, obedient to their own husbands, that the word of God be not blasphemed.

These verses clearly show that moral character needs to be modeled by older men and women. These behaviors not only become a valuable teaching tool to the younger but also honor God's word.

Likewise, Peter addresses a message to the elders. In 1 Peter 5:1–4, he says,

The elders which are among you I exhort, who am also an elder, and a witness of the sufferings of Christ, and also a partaker of the glory that shall be revealed: Feed the flock of God which is among you, taking the oversight thereof, not by constraint, but willingly; not for filthy lucre but of a ready mind; Neither as being lords over God's heritage, but being ensamples to the flock. And when the chief Shepherd shall appear, ye shall receive a crown of glory that fadeth not away.

These elders, from a scriptural point of view, are those that are mature in their faith as well as being the older or seniors. They were to feed and watch over the flock. Their responsibilities were not about personal gain or lording over the flock but being examples for them.

Age plays such an important role in God's plan for the betterment of the human race. Honestly, I suppose what makes the golden years richer than ever is using the longevity of life that we have been blessed with to make a better place for those that come after us. Age is a teacher, but it teaches.

Now also when I am old and greyheaded,
O God, forsake me not; until I have shewed
thy strength unto this generation,
and thy power to every one
that is to come.
—Psalm 71:18

CHAPTER 35

Overcoming

There are certainly many things one has to overcome in the mental as well as the physical realm to become good at the game of golf. It is probably safe to say those men and women who play on the professional level have somewhat reached this goal. However, if one is to stay on top of his or her game, overcoming has to be a part of the plan. Since there are so many facets to this game, it is so hard to get everything working together in sync. Being aware of this is a step in the right direction to overcoming instead of being overcome.

Golf, like life, is made up of many different parts and is full of challenges. My wife and I were watching the Humana Challenge being played in southern California. Erik Compton, who is the recipient of two heart transplants, was co-leader in that tournament at seventeen under. One of the announcers said he had an attitude of gratitude and was an inspiration of the importance of life. I guess this kind of a living example of overcoming should help us all to keep things in the right perspective. I am very appreciative of all the information that is given out on the Golf Channel to help us all enjoy and maybe play the game a little better. I look at this as being a part of helping others to overcome. The willingness to help others overcome is obvious in the golf world. The generosity shown by the players, sponsors and the LPGA and PGA just simply add to the greatness of the game.

There are so many sources in this world that can be a help to overcoming. From a spiritual standpoint, the Bible is one of those sources. The first step to overcoming is faith. First John 5:4–5 says,

> For whatsoever is born of God overcometh the world: and this is the victory that overcometh the world, even our faith. Who is he that overcometh the world, but he that believeth that Jesus is the Son of God?

Many times when the Bible talks of the world, it uses it in a bad sense as an organized system that acts as a rival against the things of God. John uses it in this way earlier in this same letter. He says in 1 John 2:15-17,

> Love not the world, neither the things that are in the world. If any man love the world, the love of the Father is not in him. For all that is in the world, the lust of the flesh, and the lust of the

eyes, and the pride of life, is not of the Father, but is of the world. And the world passeth away, and the lust thereof: but he that doeth the will of God abideth for ever.

If one is to overcome this system, faith must be put in Jesus, the Son of God, which results in being born again. This new spiritual life gives victory in a world that can overcome us. It certainly helps us to see things with a new set of eyes. Faith is the key that allows God, our Savior, to act on one's behalf. This unseen help is essential to overcoming so many of the obstacles in this fallen world. The point is overcoming is an ongoing part of life and we need to utilize all the sources that are available in facing the challenges that come our way.

Good advice in how to overcome difficult situations as we deal with others is given in Romans 12:17–21. It says,

Recompense to no man evil for evil. Provide things honest in the sight of all men. If it be possible, as much as lieth in you, live peaceably with all men. Dearly beloved, avenge not yourselves, but rather give place unto wrath: for it is written, Vengeance is mine; I will repay, saith the Lord. Therefore if thine enemy hunger, feed him; if he thirst give him drink: for in so doing thou shalt heap coals of fire on his head. Be not overcome of evil, but overcome evil with good.

This may not seem to be the way the world resolves issues, but it is God's way to be an overcomer. We must do all that is possible to live peaceable with all men. We overcome evil with good. When all human efforts fail, we must give it to the Lord, knowing that vengeance belongs to Him and He will repay.

We are so blessed to live in a world that has so many natural, as well as supernatural, sources that can play a major role in overcoming. Please remember that whatever your occupation is in life or wherever you are in life, you can be a recipient, as well as a contributor, to overcoming.

These things I have spoken unto you,
that in me ye might have peace.
In the world ye shall have tribulation:
but be of good cheer;
I have overcome the world.
—John 16:33

CHAPTER 36

Ever Learning

I have learned a lot over the years about what to do and what not to do while playing golf. The worst thing is that now I am so old I cannot remember all I have learned or do not have the strength to carry it out. In spite of what the golden years do to us, we should never give up on learning. Do not take the phrase "You cannot teach an old dog new tricks" too seriously. Giving in to this could be a step in the wrong direction. The present-day golf world has a lot of learning tools available to assist the old and the young alike. The game of golf has a teaching element about it. The more people can take advantage of what they learn by playing regularly, the better they will understand that golf is a game where you are ever learning.

Life also has a teaching element about it. I heard it said years ago that life is like a laboratory—full of trials and tests. Learning during difficult times can be very beneficial, both physically and spiritually. A careful study of the book of Job in the Bible reveals this truth.

In this book, God allowed Satan to take away Job's possessions, family, and health. But through it all, he became a living example of patience, faith, and hope. This lesson on life caused Job to cry out,

> Naked came I out of my mother's womb, and naked shall I return thither: the Lord gave, and the Lord hath taken away; blessed be the name of the Lord. In all this Job sinned not, nor charged God foolishly.
>
> —Job 1:21–22

What a statement of faith during a difficult time. It caused Job to understand and say, "Man that is born of woman is of few days, and full of trouble" (Job 14:1). The troubles that Job experienced drove him in a spiritual direction and caused him to proclaim,

> For I know that my redeemer liveth, and that he shall stand at the latter day upon the earth: And though after my skin worms destroy this body, yet in my flesh shall I see God: Whom I shall see for myself, and mine eyes shall behold, and not another; though my reins be consumed within me.
>
> —Job 19:25–27

This great man of faith, even though the devil had tried to destroy him and his friends had discouraged him, knew that his redeemer lived. He would see God and experience bodily resurrection. He knew if things were not made right now, they would be after his death. Job is such a good example of one that was ever learning in a positive way even during a difficult time.

In my years of studying the Bible, there seems to be a theme about never learning. I have thought of those that lived during the time when Christ came to this earth the first time. What an opportunity they had to learn from the greatest teacher that ever lived. Many who were closely associated with Him failed to learn from His messages and mission. In one short verse, John 14:6, Jesus tells His disciples the purpose of his first advent. He said unto Thomas, as well as the other disciples, "I am the way, the truth and the life: no man cometh unto the Father, but by me." Jesus is the way to God the Father. He is a truth that is worth acquiring, who can liberate or set us free from many things that can bring us into bondage. Jesus is life because He was not subject to death but made death subject to Him. The sad part about what Jesus was teaching is that Judas, one of the first twelve disciples called, would never learn these simple truths.

We have access today to the greatest book with the greatest message ever written. There is a lot to learn in life and it is sad to say many limit their learning. Take advantage of a book that is not only about life but also about ever learning.

This know also, that in the last days perilous times
shall come. For men shall be lovers of their own
selves, covetous, boasters, proud, blasphemers,
disobedient to parents, unthankful, unholy,
Without natural affection, trucebreakers,
false accusers, incontinent, fierce,
despisers of those that are good, traitors,
heady, highminded, lovers of pleasures
more than lovers of God; Having a form
of godliness, but denying the power
thereof: from such turn away. For of this sort
are they which creep into houses, and lead
captive silly women laden with sins, led away
with divers lusts, Ever learning, and never
able to come to the knowledge of the truth.
—2 Timothy 3:1–7

CHAPTER 37

Feeding Off Each Other

I believe this phrase comes into play more than we realize in the game of golf. If your playing partner or one in your foursome is playing well, it can inspire you to do likewise. It not only causes the mind to focus better but also gets the completive juices flowing. Positive influence can be a powerful thing on or off the golf course. It can make a change that is unknown to us. Honestly, it may not feel comfortable when someone else is playing better than we are in the sports world. But it can be beneficial if we feed off their good play.

A good place to be in life is to rejoice in others' victories. I am not sure that I have come to this place yet, but that is my desire. Victories in this life are temporal and short lived. If we can use them to drive us in a good direction, not a bad one, it is a win-win situation. This feeding process, whether on the golf course or in the world, has a mental element to it as well as a physical element. It can affect our game as well as our growth.

Physically, every spring in our yard, we always see the robins feeding their little ones after they are out of the nest and able to fly a short distance. This feeding element starts while they are still in the nest and continues until they are totally able to feed themselves. The feeding part of life that promotes growth and health is such a remarkable thing but is often taken for granted.

If you choose to believe the Genesis account of creation, and I hope you do, you see very early in the first chapter that God created humankind as male and female. He created them in his own image, blesses them, and tells them to be fruitful, multiply, and replenish the earth and subdue it. He then draws their attention to something by using the word "behold." Genesis 1:29–31 says,

> Behold, I have given you every herb bearing seed, which is upon the face of all the earth, and every tree, in the which is the fruit of a tree yielding seed; to you it shall be for meat. And to every beast of the earth, and to every fowl of the air, and to every thing that creepeth upon the earth, where in there is life, I have given every green herb for meat: and it was so. And God saw every thing that he had made, and behold, it was very good. And the evening and the morning were the sixth day.

Here is the first time the word "behold" is used in the Bible. This word is used many times throughout God's word to try to get humankind to see something. God wanted the male and female to see this remarkable feeding process that would not only provide food for them but also for all the animal life. He wanted them to see His provision and to see that it was very good.

There are so many things that depend on our Creator's feeding program. It is easy to lose sight of how dependent we all are on one of the most basic elements of life, which is food. The seeds that are embedded in so many of the fruits and vegetables that we all need to maintain life are so much about survival and reproduction. A quote I heard a long time ago said, "You can count the seeds in an apple, but you cannot count the apples in a seed." I believe that God has put many reminders in place to show us how dependent we are on Him.

We may feed off each other on the golf course, but we all are fed by the Master's hand.

For my thoughts are not your thoughts, neither are your ways my ways, saith the Lord. For as the heavens are higher than the earth, so are my ways higher than your ways, and my thoughts than your thoughts. For as the rain cometh down, and the snow from heaven, and returneth not thither, but watereth the earth, and maketh it bring forth and bud, that it may give seed to the sower, and

bread to the eater: So shall my word be that goeth
forth out of my mouth: it shall not return void,
but it shall accomplish that which I please, and
it shall prosper in the thing whereto I sent it.
—Isaiah 55:8–11

CHAPTER 38

On the Green

I heard an announcer say one time that golf is the greatest show on grass. What occurs after reaching the green can certainly make a happy or a sad ending to the show. The green not only adds another beauty to the golf course but also presents a new challenge to the best of golfers. It is a completely new game when you leave the fairway and step on the green. If you are fortunate to get there in regulation, it is a good feeling that may result in a birdie. The power of the drive and the well-placed iron shots suddenly diminish into the precision of putting. I believe that putting gets as much or more attention than any other shot on the golf course. I, for one, really enjoy watching the precision putting of Jordan Spieth. This only makes the show more enjoyable. The greens are the focal point of the game and where the outcome is determined. What takes place on the last green plays a major role in the greatest show on grass.

Outcomes hinge on so many things, whether on or off the golf course. Our choices and decisions can be a deciding factor in whether we win or lose. In my life, I have come to the conclusion that I need more help than I can get in the physical sense if I expect to have a good ending. The written word of God is so available in America but it is so neglected by many. It is a source of information that can help us when we are winning or losing in life. Believing and valuing its message and identifying with what it teaches can help us make good choices and decisions based upon a book that is spiritual. Paul, in his closing words to the church at Ephesus, tells the Christians if they are to be strong in the Lord they must put on the whole armor of God. Part of this armor is the sword of the spirit, which is the word of God.

In order to stand against the evilness of this world and have a good ending in the game of life, God's word is essential. A good ending is echoed in 2 Timothy 4:6–8, where Paul writes,

> For I am now ready to be offered, and the time of my departure is at hand. I have fought a good fight, I have finished my course, I have kept the faith: Henceforth there is laid up for me a crown of righteousness, which the Lord, the righteousness judge, shall give me at that day: and not to me only, but unto all them also that love his appearing.

Paul uses three figures of speech for a good ending. He uses a military figure (fighting a good fight), an athletic figure (finishing the course), and a religious figure (keeping the faith). Paul knew that he would be rewarded one day as well as others who kept the faith and has a love for the second appearing of Jesus Christ.

The words of Christ, in his prayer in the gospel of John, show us something else that makes for a good ending. He said in John 17:4–5,

> I have glorified thee on the earth: I have finished the work which thou gavest me to do. And now, O Father, glorify thou me with thine own self with the glory which I had with thee before the world was.

Jesus glorified the Father by showing His power, compassion, love, and forgiveness. The Father would glorify Jesus through His resurrection and ascension back to heaven from where He came. If we are willing to exercise faith in Jesus and start following Him scripturally, we too can glorify God by showing Christ's love, compassion, and forgiveness to others. From a scripture point of view, we can read time and time again of good endings. We can also read time and time again how to end good in this life.

Ending well on the golf course is determined many times on the green. In like manner, ending well in life is determined by what we do with the one that came to give life and give it more abundantly.

> Search the scriptures, for in them ye think ye
> have eternal life: and they are they which
> testify of me.
> —John 5:39

CHAPTER 39

The Caddie

I have never had the privilege of having a caddie, except when my wife and I are on a golf date and she will hand me a club or putter. It is very evident from a professional level of golf that the caddie plays an important role in the success of the golfer. The golfer and the caddie picture a two-person team that works together for a common goal, namely winning. I have heard and seen, while watching many hours of golf on television, that many of these two-person teams have worked together for years and developed a very special relationship. The communication between them is not only enjoyable to hear as a spectator but is essential for standing in the winner's circle. Recently I heard Jordan Spieth talking, right after he had won the 2015 US Open, about how he and his caddie work together as a team.

It is very important for us to express verbally how important the team members are, whether in golf or many other things in life that require teamwork.

Those on the second string play an important role in practicing as well as the success of the team as a whole, whether it is a group of people or a two-person team. Verbal communication, encouragement, and appreciation are such a step in the right direction.

When you read the first account of humankind in the Bible, you see God started out with a two-person team. In chapter 1 of Genesis, we have the account of God creating the planet Earth and making it inhabitable and suitable for the first two-person team to live on. This first team was male and female. They were to be fruitful, multiply and replenish the earth, and have dominion over all the other created things. From this first male and female team, marriage would be instituted. Jesus confirmed this truth when He was being tempted by the Pharisees concerning whether it was lawful for a man to put away his wife. In Matthew 19:4–6, he said,

> Have ye not read, that he which made them at the beginning made them male and female, And said, For this cause shall a man leave father and mother, and shall cleave to his wife: and they twain shall be one flesh? Wherefore they are no more twain, but one flesh. What therefore God hath joined together, let not man put asunder.

The book of Hebrews tells us this kind of marriage is honorable. Hebrews 13:4 says, "Marriage is honorable in all, and the bed undefiled: but whoremongers and adulterers God will judge."

A family would come from the first male and female team. What a blessing our families are to us. I always enjoy seeing those who play professional golf with their families after they have finished their round and are waiting to receive a trophy or be in a playoff. This is a public testimony of how important their families and loved ones are to them. Families that live, work, love, laugh, cry, talk, and pray together make up the greatest teams on earth.

After fifty-one years of marriage to my wife, Darlene, our team is smaller in our home now. It is larger outside our home since we now have two beautiful granddaughters: Mikhaila and Sydney. Lord willing, maybe the team will get bigger in the days to come. A newborn baby is a welcome addition to the family team.

The secret to our being on the same team for fifty-one years is, in order, Christ, communication, and consideration.

This formula will work for any team.

Except the Lord build the house, they labour in vain
that build it: except the Lord keep the city,
the watchman waketh but in vain. It is vain for you
to rise up early, to sit up late, to
eat the bread of sorrows:
for so he giveth his beloved sleep. Lo, children are an

heritage of the Lord: and the fruit of the womb is
his reward. As arrows are in the
hand of a mighty man;
so are children of the youth. Happy is the man that
hath his quiver full of them: thy
shall not be ashamed,
but they shall speak with the enemies in the gate.
—Psalm 127:1–5

CHAPTER 40

Being Honest

Golf is a game that asks us to be honest. It might be better to say that it promotes honesty on as well as off the course. A game that enhances integrity is a plus for society. It is always noble when you see someone on the professional level call for an official at the expense of losing a stroke. Golf gives opportunities for honesty but also allows for dishonesty since you find yourself in places on the course where no one else is watching. From a human point of view, this is where temptation can come into play.

A story is told of a little boy who was playing in the pantry just before dinner. He had gotten the cookie jar down and his mother heard him. She said, "Willie, what are you doing?" He answered, "I am fighting temptation." Whether young or old, we all seem to have to fight temptation.

The Bible says in 1 Corinthians 10:13,

> There hath no temptation taken you but such as is common to man: but God is faithful, who

will not suffer you to be tempted above that ye are able; but will with the temptation also make a way to escape, that ye may be able to bear it.

All humankind deals with temptation. The good news is God is faithful during this time and will not allow you to be tempted beyond what you are able to bear. We cannot avoid temptation but the Lord can make a way of escape. A relationship with God through Jesus Christ adds a new dimension to life. It can help us in dealing with the many temptations of life that come in all shapes and sizes. Being mindful of the Lord's presence and understanding our responsibilities to Him can enhance truthfulness and honesty. A good prayer that we all should pray each day is "Lead us not into temptation and deliver us from evil." There are so many things that develop honesty as well as try to destroy it. There is a God-given faculty within us that is designed by our Creator to foster honesty. It is the conscience. The first active conscience in humankind is seen in the third chapter of Genesis. After Adam and Eve sinned and disobeyed God, a consciousness was awakened within them to know good and evil.

A good conscience is only one of the helps that we have to develop honesty. Strong parental and educational instruction, plus biblical instruction, is a good starting point. Paul makes a good general statement about honesty in Romans 12:17, "Recompense to no man evil for evil. Provide things honest in the sight of all men."

If people can conduct themselves in an honest, noble way in the sight of others, they become an advocate for honesty. God's word is not only a source of information on honesty but is a truth that can liberate us from so many things that try to dominate, damage, or destroy us. Jesus said to the Jews who believed on Him, "If ye continue in my word, then are ye my disciples indeed; and ye shall know the truth and the truth shall make you free" (John 8:31–32).

A continual study of God's word will help us identify and experience truth in a deeper way. This truth helps deliver us from lies and deceptions and can be an engine that drives us to honesty in all walks of life.

Everyone seems to win from honest behavior, whether they are playing golf or playing in the game called life.

Let us walk honestly, as in the day;
not in rioting and drunkenness, not in chambering
and wantonness, not in strife and envying.
But put ye on the Lord Jesus Christ,
and make not provision for the flesh,
to fulfil the lusts thereof.
—Romans 13:13–14

CHAPTER 41

Big Is Not Always Better

It is very entertaining to see the golfers of small stature bombing the ball out there like their competitors of larger stature. Size may make a difference in some sports, but golf seems to be an exception to the rule. Swing patterns and club speed seem to put most players on a level playing field regardless of how big they are. This is another reason golf can be a game for anyone. It does not discriminate because of one's size. Size certainly gets a lot of attention in this modern world we live in. As the electronic world has evolved, it seems like the most sought-out devices of communication have gotten smaller. One of my golfing buddies, Ron Fleming, has a wristwatch that will tell the distance to the hole on each shot.

As a boy growing up in Calhoun County, West Virginia, size always got my attention. I always wanted to be big and strong like my dad: Lloyd Yoak. Even at the one-room school I attended for eight years, size always came into play when choosing up to play ball.

We little guys could always expect to be chosen last. But as the years have unfolded, physical size no longer gets much of my attention. The good Lord has made those He created in His own image different in shapes, sizes, and color. If we understand and believe this, we should try the best we can to reflect His image.

In the opening verses of Hebrews, the writer tells us that God has revealed Himself through His Son. Hebrews 1:1–3 says,

> God, who at sundry times and in divers manners spake in time past unto the fathers by the prophets, Hath in these last days spoken unto us by his Son, whom he hath appointed heir of all things, by whom also he made the worlds; Who being the brightness of his glory, and the express image of his person, and upholding all things by the word of his power, when he had by himself purged our sins, sat down on the right hand of the Majesty on high;

This scripture reminds us that God has spoken to humankind in various ways down through the ages. But in the last day, He has spoken to us, revealed, and reflected Himself to us through His Son, Jesus. Christ was the express image of God or the exact representation of Him. The more we study and learn about Jesus Christ, the more we can reflect the image of our Creator.

From a scriptural point of view, it is safe to say that Christ did not discriminate against size. When you read the account of the conversion of Saul of Tarsus in Acts 9, you see he was confronted by the risen Christ and commissioned to be a chosen vessel to bear the name of Christ to the Gentiles, kings, and the children of Israel. Later on, Saul's name was changed to Paul, which means "little." This man may have been small in stature but he was mighty spiritually. He wrote thirteen of the twenty-seven books in the New Testament. His writings have played a major role in the hearts of millions down through the ages. Size can make a difference, but the Lord can use all sizes.

When Samuel, the priest and prophet, was sent to Bethlehem to the house of Jesse to select and anoint a new king to be over Israel, the Lord told him in 1 Samuel 16:7,

> Look not on his countenance, or on the height of his stature; because I have refused him: for the Lord seeth not as man seeth; for man looketh on the outward appearance, but the Lord looketh on the heart.

Within this verse, we see the Lord does not base His choices or selection on appearance or size but on what is in the heart. The heart matters more to the Lord than size.

Society may want to look at size, but for the believer in Christ, we need to focus on the size of God. This will help us keep the problems of life in perspective. I had a brother in the Lord who was dealing with a lot of physical difficulties tell me he had to keep focusing on the size of God, not the size of the problems. Seeing problems, as well as people, through the eyes of faith is a step in the right direction. Faith does not discriminate when it comes to size.

And Jesus entered and passed through Jericho.
And, behold, there was a man named Zacchaeus.
Which was the chief among the publicans, and
he was rich. And he sought to see Jesus who
he was; and could not for the press, because
he was little of stature. And he ran before, and
climbed up into a sycomore tree to see him:
for he was to pass that way. And when Jesus came
to the place, he looked up, and saw him, and said
unto him, Zacchaeus, make haste, and come down;
for today I must abide at thy house. And he made
haste, and came down, and received him joyfully.
—Luke 19:1–6

CHAPTER 42

A Work in Progress

More than once, I have heard professional golfers talk about the hard work they have put into their game. You hear phrases like "The hard work is paying off," especially if they have just won a tournament or have finished well. I think we all would agree that golf is a work in progress. Progress fits very well with golf, since it is a game about advancing or moving the ball forward. From a personal standpoint, I have worked on my game in a feeble but enjoyable way for fifty-plus years and I still have problems advancing or moving the ball forward the way I would like to. So goes the phrase "Practice makes perfect." Honestly, from an amateur perspective, using work in relationship to golf is a stretch of the imagination. On the other hand, it is obvious that the men and women in the professional golf world work hard to perform at the highest level. This ongoing work ethic is not only rewarded but should be commended by all that benefits from it. Their hard work is touching many people who will probably never pick up a golf club.

A good work ethic is a learned behavior and should be taught at a young age as well as rewarded for a job well done. Work should be an enjoyable experience as well as a satisfying experience. Work was a part of the perfect world we read about in Genesis 2:7–9, ...15.

> And the Lord God formed man of the dust of the ground, and breathed into his nostrils the breath of life; and man became a living soul. And the Lord God planted a garden eastward in Eden; and there he put the man whom he had formed. And out of the ground made the Lord God to grow every tree that is pleasant to the sight, and good for food; the tree of life also in the midst of the garden, and the tree of knowledge of good and evil ... And the Lord God took the man, and put him into the Garden of Eden to dress it and to keep it.

Within this scripture, we have the account of God forming man from the dust of the ground and then planting a garden in Eden and putting man in it to care for it. This first work assignment given to man not only shows the mind of God in relationship to work but also the intention of God in relationship to work. God intended for humankind to work in this perfect environment that He created for them. After they failed in obeying God and were driven from this Garden of Eden, the enjoyable work experience would become burdensome. Due to the curse God would pronounce upon the earth sorrow, sweat, thorns, and thistles would have to be dealt with as they tried to survive in a fallen world. Suddenly everything would become less enjoyable. Even the fellowship they had with their Creator, who walked and talked with them in the cool of the evening, would no longer be the same.

Whether one chooses to believe it or not, fellowship with God our Creator is so important in all walks of life. It can give us a new outlook on life and can only be recognized and appreciated when there is a relationship with God through faith in Christ. The cross of Christ bridged the gap between God and humankind so one can experience new life in a new way.

Fellowship with God is again possible if the Lord is in the picture and the plan. Even work can be so much more meaningful and enjoyable. Psalm 127:1–2, tells us,

> Except the Lord build the house, they labour in vain that build it: except the Lord keep the city, the watchman waketh in vain. It is vain for you to rise up early, to sit up late, to eat the bread of sorrows: for so he giveth his beloved sleep.

The thought here seems to be that human effort is vain in building, watching, and working if the Lord is not in it. From a scripture point of view, the Lord wants not only to be a part of our work, but He also wants to work on the one who believes and trusts in Him by faith. This too is a work in progress that is designed to advance or move the believer forward.

Being confident of this very thing,
that he which hath begun a good work in you
will perform it until the day of Jesus Christ.
—Philippians 1:6

CHAPTER 43

Forgiving

The golf clubs that I am now playing with are the MacGregor Senior Flex with graphite shafts. One of the selling points was that these clubs are more forgiving and the salesman was sure they would lower my score. The sales pitch worked, but the lower score is questionable. In defense of the sales pitch, golf clubs are designed to be more forgiving. I am all for every ounce of ingenuity and technology that can be put into making it easier for the golfer. At least the golf clubs should have a forgiving quality, since so many of the other facets of the game can be very unforgiving. The trees along the fairways, water hazards, and sand traps are all a part of the mix. I once heard an announcer talking about the grass in the rough being so unforgiving. It would grab the club and make it very difficult to get the club under the ball. Golf clubs that are designed to be forgiving are very important to the golfer.

Likewise, it is very important that we all understand that God has designed humankind to be forgiven and forgiving. The benefits of having golf clubs that are forgiving are small compared to a person with a forgiving heart. All through the pages of the Bible, it shows us a God that is our Creator and Savior and shows Him as being very forgiving. Psalm 86:5 says, "For thou Lord, are good, and ready to forgive; and plenteous in mercy unto all them that call upon thee."

David saw the Lord ready to forgive since humankind is the only creation of God that is made in His image. A forgiving spirit should be a part of our makeup. Like our Creator, we should be ready to forgive. Our motivation for forgiving others should be because God has made a way for us to be forgiven through Jesus Christ. Paul echoes this truth in Ephesians 4:32 when he says, "And be ye kind one to another, tenderhearted, forgiving one another, even as God for Christ's sake hath forgiven you."

Many things can drive us or motivate us in life. If one is willing to consider what the Lord has done and is doing for us, it can be a plus in our relationships with others, whether it is at home, work, or play. The value of forgiveness as well as the benefits of it make all the difference in the world. From a scriptural vantage point, one's willingness to forgive others is not to be taken lightly. Jesus said these words in Matthew 6:14–15:

> For if ye forgive men their trespasses, your heavenly Father will also forgive you; But if ye

forgive not men their trespasses, neither will your Father forgive your trespasses.

I believe these words of Jesus show the seriousness and importance of forgiving. One's willingness to see a personal forgiveness is such a step in the right direction and can add a new dimension to life.

A common theme throughout the pages of the Bible is the sin of humankind. God Himself is the one that put in place a perfect plan to have sin forgiven and covered. David understood this truth in Psalm 32:1–2, when he said,

Blessed is he whose transgression is forgiven, whose sin is covered. Blessed is the man unto whom the Lord imputeth not iniquity, and in whose spirit there is no guile.

These verses are about the blessedness or happiness of forgiveness. Three statements express what brings happiness.

1. The one whose sin is forgiven—carried away.
2. The one whose sin is covered—an act of atonement.
3. The one whose sin is not imputed to them—it is not counted against them.

God's perfect plan for forgiveness is seen throughout the pages of the Old Testament and finalized in the

New Testament where we learn of the incarnation (the embodiment of God in the human form of Jesus). Through Jesus Christ, forgiveness is offered to "whosoever will."

The same way forgiving and unforgiving is a part of the game of golf, it is also a part of the game of life. It can be difficult, but it is doable if one is motivated morally and spiritually. Even though golf clubs are more forgiving today, we still have to practice to hit them properly. Practicing forgiveness is a win-win for anyone.

> Then came Peter to him, and said, Lord,
> how oft shall my brother sin against me
> and I forgive Him? till seven times?
> Jesus saith unto him, I say not unto thee,
> Until seven times: but, Until seventy times seven.
> —Matthew 18:21–22

CHAPTER 44

Give It a Chance

Since golf is a game where most players have a tendency to talk to themselves, verbally or mentally, why not incorporate the little phrase "Give it a chance" into one's vocabulary every time the putter is picked up? From a personal standpoint, my putts come up short so much of the time. They do not have a chance. In knowing that a three-foot putt is as important as a three-hundred-yard drive, anything I can do verbally or mentally to get the ball to the hole or at least past it I will do it. The last time my wife went with me on a practice round, I noticed her reminding me to give it a chance. A verbal reminder, whether expressed personally or by someone else, can be so beneficial on the golf course as well as life in general. Words are very productive when spoken in the right way at the right time. They not only benefit the speaker but also can promote good. Proverbs 15:23 says it best. "A man hath joy by the answer of his mouth: and a word spoken in due season, how good is it!" There should be an inward satisfaction or joy from our words or speech as well as an outward benefit to others.

Proper speech is certainly commended throughout the word of God. A careful study of the Bible shows us that speech, speak, spoken, tongue, and mouth so much of the time center around humankind's words. Our words not only act as a reminder but can reveal our character. Jesus said in Matthew 12:33–37,

> Either make the tree good, and his fruit good; or else make the tree corrupt, and his fruit corrupt: for the tree is known by his fruit. O generation of vipers, how can ye, being evil, speak good things? for out of the abundance of the heart the mouth speaketh. A good man out of the good treasure of the heart bringeth forth good things; and an evil man out of the evil treasure bringeth forth evil things. But I say unto you, That every idle word that men shall speak, they shall give account thereof in the day of judgment. For by thy words thou shalt be justified, and by thy words thou shalt be condemned.

The same way that fruit shows the condition of the tree, words show the condition of the heart. Careless or idle words can haunt a person at the judgment. For anyone who is willing to believe this, it should be an eye-opener when it comes to opening the mouth.

A statement that I read a long time ago said, "There are two things that are bad for the heart: running up stairs and running down people." In Colossians 4:6, Paul gives some good advice to the saints and faithful brethren in Christ when he tells them, "Let your speech be always with grace, seasoned with salt, that ye may know how ye ought to answer every man."

Two things should characterize the speech of a believer.

1. Their words should be gracious, not hurtful or harsh.
2. Their words should be salty, marked with purity or tasteful.

Words characterized this way are the proper way to answer every man. Proverbs 16:23–24 says, "The heart of the wise teaches his mouth, and addeth learning to his lips. Pleasant words are as an honeycomb, sweet to the soul, and health to the bones." The wise in heart should teach oneself in relationship to words and instructions. The writer of this proverb makes so many connections between words and everyday life.

The four little words "Give it a chance" may be a self-reminder on the golf course and the many words we utter day by day should be a reminder of who we are and whose we are.

Let the words of my mouth, and the meditation
of my heart, be acceptable in thy sight,
O Lord, my strength, and my redeemer.
—Psalm 19:14

CHAPTER 45

Anger

Have I ever gotten angry on the golf course? Yes. Did it help my game? No. My anger was not directed at others but at myself. Anger that is expressed against others or shown in a visible way surely takes away from any sporting event. Golf should be an exception to the rule and by large seems to be. There is so much beauty to be seen while playing or watching golf, so why allow anger to destroy this for yourself or others? Throwing clubs and foul language take so much away from a game that provides a great opportunity to build character and integrity in the lives of young people. I hope that those who make the rules that govern the game of golf will always keep this game family friendly, even if it means a loss of strokes or a fine for those that tarnish the image of this great game. In this day and age that we are a part of so much gets more visible as time unfolds. Knowing that someone is always watching should help each of us to control our emotions as well as bite our tongue when things do not go the way we think they should. Recently while watching a golf tournament, I heard an announcer apologizing to the listening audience if they were offended by something that was said after a bad shot.

A competitive spirit has a good side to it as well as a bad side if we allow it to say and do things without thinking. Since anger seems to get more attention sometimes than good behavior, it seems logical that we all need to try to manage it in some way or the other.

From a personal standpoint or Christian point of view, I try to allow temptations and difficult times to drive me to the word of God. Psalm 119:11 says, "Thy word have I hid in my heart, that I might not sin against thee." If God's Word is hidden in our heart, it is like oil to a car and good diet to the body. It is not only preventive maintenance but it can also help us manage or control situations that may hurt others or us. God's word is a guideline that can shed a new light during times of darkness. Psalm 119:105 says, "Thy word is a lamp unto my feet, and a light unto my path." Man-made light only allows us to see so far, but God's word gives us illumination for the present while shining into the future. The light of God's word is a good source of information on anger and how to manage it. The gospel of John gives an example of what many see as a righteous anger shown by Jesus Christ. John 2:13–17 says,

And the Jews' Passover was at hand, and Jesus went up to Jerusalem, And found in the temple those that sold oxen and sheep and doves, and the changers of money sitting: And when he had made a scourge of small cords, he drove them all out of the temple, and the sheep, and the oxen; and poured out the changers' money, and overthrew the tables; and said unto them that sold doves, Take these things hence; make not my Father's house an house of merchandise. And his disciples remembered that it was written, The zeal of thine house hath eaten me up.

I have always thought this anger was provoked because Jesus was trying to guard God's interest. He was showing a zeal for God's house that was being changed into a house for selling merchandise. Later on in the ministry of Christ, He would find this situation had gotten even worse and He again would cleanse the temple. This time after casting out those who sold and bought in the temple, He even threw out the tables of the moneychangers and the seats of those that sold doves as He said, "It is written, my house shall be called the house of prayer, but ye have made it a den of thieves." This righteous anger was justified because the one who was angry was the God of Israel in the flesh, who was provoked to anger many times because of the sin and disobedience of His own people.

The prophet Isaiah shows us one of the many times they provoked the Holy One of Israel to anger when he said,

> Hear, O heavens, and give ear, O earth; for the Lord hath spoken, I have nourished and brought up children, and they have rebelled against me. The ox knoweth his owner, and the ass his master's crib; but Israel doth not know, my people doth not consider. Ah sinful nation, a people laden with iniquity, a seed of evil doers, children that are corrupters: they have forsaken the Lord, they have provoked the Holy One of Israel unto anger, they are gone away backward.
>
> —Isaiah 1:2–4

The dumbest of the animals knew who their owners were, in contrast to God's people who had forgotten Him. This incited anger in their Lord, who according to Psalm 103:8 is merciful, gracious, and slow to anger. God's word not only shows what angers our Creator and Savior, but it also gives good advice on how to control it.

Proverbs 15:1 is an excellent source of information on anger. It says, "A soft answer turneth away wrath: but grievous words stir up anger." A soft answer kills verbal violence as well as controls anger. Another scripture that I have found helpful in managing anger is found in Ephesians 4:26, which says, "Be ye angry and sin not; let not the sun go down upon your wrath." What this says to me is to get rid of anger quickly. I had written in my Bible years ago that anger is one letter short of danger.

Misguided anger, whether on the golf course or off, is not pretty, pleasant, or productive.

He that is soon angry dealeth foolishly:
and a man of wicked devices is hated.
—Proverbs 14:17

CHAPTER 46

A Pathway Out

It is always interesting and entertaining to watch the professional golfers thread the ball through trees to get it back into play or on the green. It is probably not entertaining for them, but it is for the spectators. They always seem to find the right way out. There always seems to be a lot of thought put into these challenging shots by the players and the caddies. Obstacles that challenge one's skills form another facet of the game where one is ever learning. I heard said a long time ago that a life of ease is not a good teacher.

If one is willing to be teachable, it can shed a new light on or give a new perspective, even during difficult situations. The writer in Psalm 119:71 boldly says, "It is good for me that I have been afflicted; that I might learn thy statutes." The writer of the psalm understood that difficult times and adversity drove him to the Lord and His word. It made him teachable. He used the situation that he found himself in as a pathway to learning. Finding a pathway out on a golf course means utilizing the mind, playing skills, and getting good counsel from others. The counsel or advice we can receive from God's word is much needed in our society today.

I feel the pathway out to so many problems that we all deal with from time to time can be found in God's word. That is the reason it is so important to look into the perfect Law of Liberty (Bible) and continue in it being not a forgetful hearer but a doer of the work. James 1:25 says this man or individual shall be blessed in his deeds. So many times, it seems to take problems or difficulties in our lives for us to seek God's pathway out. God's word is nondiscriminatory and shows us the paths of life whether good or bad. Within His word, we see the result of going down the wrong path. But the good news is the Bible shows us a path where we can experience victory regardless of what we have to deal with in this life. First John 5:4–5 says,

> For whatsoever is born of God overcometh the world: and this is the victory that overcometh the world, even our faith. Who is he that overcometh the world, but he that believeth that Jesus is the Son of God?

Did you notice in this verse that faith is our pathway out to victory if we believe God's word? Unfortunately, so many go through life and never exercise faith in Christ. The world we are all a part of seems to throw a lot of good and bad at us. Overcoming these rests in our faith in Jesus Christ. He has made us an escape from the downfalls from a life of ease as well as a life of difficulties.

I feel the writer of Proverbs had a good handle on the good and the bad of life. He said in Proverbs 30:7–9,

> Two things have I required of thee; deny me them not before I die: Remove far from me vanity and lies; give me neither poverty nor riches; feed me with food convenient for me; Lest I be full, and deny thee, and say, Who is the Lord? Or lest I be poor, and steal, and take the name of my God in vain.

This writer understood that too much in life, as well as too little, can be detrimental to one's spiritual well-being. I thoroughly believe that our faith in Christ and following Him scripturally can help us keep materialistic things in balance. Likewise, it can show us a pathway out to escape those things that can be dangerous to us physically and spiritually.

The games we play and enjoy in life have obstacles we have to overcome if we are going to win. Even the game itself can become an obstacle to overcoming the world if the Lord is not in the equation.

Spiritually speaking, the Lord Himself has provided us the ultimate pathway out.

Hast thou not known? hast thou not heard, that the
everlasting God, the Lord, the Creator of the ends of
the earth, fainteth not, neither is weary?
There is no searching of his understanding.
He giveth power to the faint; and to them
that have no might he increaseth strength.
Even the youths shall faint and be weary,
and the young men shall utterly fall: But they that
wait upon the Lord shall renew their strength;
they shall mount up with wings as eagles;
they shall run, and not be weary;
and they shall walk, and not faint.
—Isaiah 40:28–31

CHAPTER 47

Finishing Well

Just how important is finishing well on the golf course? Very much in every way. Even though one might start out playing poorly, a good finish seems to do something for us who love to play the game. It builds momentum for the next round and seems to boost one's confidence, regardless of one's playing level. From my perspective, good shots plus a good attitude while having a good time is a recipe for a good finish on the golf course, whether playing the game as a livelihood or just recreational. This may not be a natural ability for many people but can be a step in the right direction. Good shots means working on your game, while a good attitude and a good time hinge on how one looks at things in the big picture.

Life is made up of many different parts. When we can see our part of life, being small compared to what others may be dealing with, this should foster an attitude of gratitude. Just being thankful for health and the God-given abilities we have adds to a good finish. Finishing well on the golf course, along with the many other parts of life, is very important but not at the expense of finishing well spiritually. It is very important to understand from a scriptural prospective that humanity has a spiritual part to it. Humanity, unlike all other things God created, was made in His image. God's existence is always assumed throughout the Bible. He is eternal and everlasting to everlasting based upon this scriptural assumption.

It is safe to say that all humankind has an eternal spirit that is destined to live on eternally. It is sobering to think that the Bible only gives two choices when it comes to eternity: heaven or hell. I believe these two places are somewhat shown in the words of Jesus when He spoke of two men who died in Luke 16:19–31.

> There was a certain rich man, which was clothed in purple and fine linen, and fared sumptuously every day: And there was a certain beggar named Lazarus, which was laid at his gate, full of sores, And desiring to be fed with the crumbs which fell from the rich man's table: moreover the dogs came and licked his sores. And it came to pass, that the beggar died, and was carried by the angels into Abraham's bosom: the rich man also died, and was buried; And in hell he lift up his eyes, being in torments, and seeth Abraham afar off, and Lazarus in his boson. And he cried and said, Father Abraham, have

mercy on me, and send Lazarus, that he may dip the tip of his finger in water, and cool my tongue; for I am tormented in this flame. But Abraham said, Son, remember that thou in thy lifetime receivedst thy good things, and likewise Lazarus evil things: but now he is comforted, and thou art tormented. And beside all this, between us and you there is a great gulf fixed: so that they which would pass from hence to you cannot; neither can they pass to us, that would come from thence. Then he said, I pray thee therefore, father, that thou wouldest send him to my father's house: For I have five brethren; that he may testify unto them, lest they also come into this place of torment. Abraham saith unto him, They have Moses and the prophets; let them hear them. And he said, Nay, father Abraham; but if one went unto them from the dead, they will repent. And he said unto him, If they hear not Moses and the prophets, neither will they be persuaded, though one rose from the dead.

In this scripture, hell is a place of separation and suffering. A place where memories will persist as well as a place one can never escape. The good news is the other place is synonymous with heaven in that it is a place of comfort, peace, and rest under the care of Abraham. I believe it is obvious who finished well in these words that Jesus spoke.

Paul, who was probably the most spiritual man second to Jesus Christ, relates in a personal way how to finish well. Shortly before his own death, he wrote these words in 1 Timothy 4:6–8:

> For I am now ready to be offered, and the time of my departure is at hand. I have fought a good fight, I have finished my course, I have kept the faith: Henceforth there is laid up for me a crown of righteousness, which the Lord, the righteous judge, shall give me at that day: and not to me only, but unto all them also that love his appearing.

To finish well, Paul knew that one must put up a good fight while keeping the faith, which would result in a reward for all those who would love the second coming of Christ. He clearly understood the importance of finishing well spiritually, knowing that humankind, who is made in the image of God, has a spiritual element that needs developed and nurtured.

Paul echoes these truths in his writing to the church at Thessalonica. In 1 Thessalonians 5:21–23, he said,

> Prove all things; hold fast that which is good. Abstain from all appearance of evil. And the very God of peace sanctify you wholly; and I pray God your whole spirit and soul and body be preserved blameless unto the coming of our Lord Jesus Christ.

The footnote in my study Bible says "that man is a tri-unity of soul, body and spirit patterned in a sense after the divine Godhead, in whose image he was both created and made."[1] God's word is such a valuable tool that helps us to identify who we are and is an excellent source of information on finishing well, on or off the golf course.

> His Lord said unto him,
> Well done, good and faithful servant;
> thou hast been faithful over a few things,
> I will make thee ruler over many things:
> enter thou into the joy of thy lord.
> —Matthew 25:23

CHAPTER 48

Limitations

Age, I suppose, is probably one of the most common things that limits us on the golf course. When I got in my midsixties, I certainly started noticing I was not as strong as I used to be. The shots started getting shorter and it was not as easy to walk eighteen holes of golf. Age can do many things to us, but it has not erased my desire to play. If we just laugh off our limitations, it will make life better on or off the golf course. Limitations seem to be woven into the fabric of the game of golf. There is only a certain amount of clubs and putters available for use, plus the limitations that are experienced on the fairways, greens, and sand traps challenge the players personally and put everyone on a level playing field. There seems to be a bad side as well as a good side to limitations, whether we ever give it much thought or not. Limitations are good for our own well-being. Our Creator designed many of them. The darkness, light, sunshine, rain, and the seasons were all limited for the benefit of humankind. The bad side of limitations is when we close our minds and just accept the status quo. This can cause us to limit ourselves. It is beneficial at times to think outside the box. One time I saw a cartoon of a cat sitting next to its litter box and looking very ashamed. The owner was standing sternly over the cat and pointing his finger at the cat, saying, "Never think outside the box again." This may be good advice to a cat but not to us humans. Our thinking and feelings can get us into trouble sometimes. We cannot really prevent thoughts, but we need to understand that our minds can limit us and take us in the wrong direction.

Since coming to the Lord many years ago, I have seen and experienced the importance of trying to align our thinking with God's word. The more we can incorporate the teachings of the Bible into our everyday life, the less chance we have of limiting God's involvement in our lives. Yes, God wants to be involved in the lives of those created in His image. A study of the Old Testament clearly shows how He wanted to be involved in the nation of Israel, His chosen people. It also shows how they limited themselves by rebelling against God's revelation to them. They simply shot themselves in the foot time and time again by refusing God's instructions. They aligned themselves with ungodly nations and attached themselves to false gods and teachings, which led to God's judgment.

Scripture teaches that God does not take pleasure in judgment. The prophet Ezekiel echoes this truth in his words to the house of Israel. He said in Ezekiel 18:30–32,

> Therefore I will judge you, O house of Israel, every one according to his ways, saith the Lord God. Repent, and turn yourselves from all your transgressions; so iniquity shall not be your ruin. Cast away from you all your transgressions, whereby ye have transgressed; and make you a new heart and a new spirit: for why will ye die, O house of Israel? For I have no pleasure in the death of him that dieth, saith the Lord God: wherefore turn yourselves, and live ye.

God was asking these people to repent or turn away from and have a change of mind about their sins. God did not take pleasure in judging them according to their ways. The good news is God's word shows us what God has pleasure in or what is pleasing to Him. Psalm 147:11 says, "The Lord taketh pleasure in them that fear him, in those that hope in his mercy."

The point here is that limitations can be self-inflicted if we ignore God's word, ways, and warnings. The Lord has a plan for this world that He created and loves. A careful study of His plan reveals that there is a fix for all of the limitations of humanity. It may not come in this life, but rest assured it will come in the life that Christ promises all who are willing to repent and receive Him as Savior. Don't ever lose hope because of your limitations on or off the golf course. Just try to do what the old gospel song says. "Trust and obey for there is no other way to be happy in Jesus, but to trust and obey."[4]

> Trust in the Lord, and do good; so shalt thou dwell in
> the land, and verily thou shalt be fed.
> Delight thyself also in the Lord; and he
> shall give thee the desires of the heart.
> Commit thy way unto the Lord;
> trust also in him; and he shall bring
> it to pass. And he shall bring forth thy
> righteousness as the light, and thy
> judgment as the noonday.
> —Psalm 37:3–6

CHAPTER 49

Get Over It

I don't know if anyone ever played a perfect round of golf. If you are an exception to the rule, this chapter may not be for you. Wherever life has taken you and whatever you are doing, most likely you are dealing with disappointments in one way or the other. To dwell on these can be detrimental to the present as well as the future. It certainly can foster anger publicly as well as personally. Bad decisions, shots, or score cards can be disappointing on the links, but the good news is the next round may be the starting point for getting over it. Time seems to have a way of erasing our hurts and disappointments if we allow it. I believe it is very unhealthy for us to carry around a baggage of disappointments, hurts, and hard feelings. Some way or another, we have to get rid of this weight or it will hinder our progression, rob us of joy, and destroy relationships. One thing that I have learned from studying God's word is that the Lord wants us to progress physically as well as spiritually. I believe the latter has a greater effect on us than the former. If one is willing to feed and nurture the spiritual part of us, it is a step in the right direction.

First Peter 2:1–2 says,

> Wherefore laying aside all malice, and all guile, and hypocrisies, and envies, and all evil speaking, As newborn babes, desire the sincere milk of the word, that ye may grow there by.

These verses are pretty self-explanatory; we need to lay aside bad behavior that can hinder or stunt our spiritual growth and desire God's word as a newborn baby desires milk. Growing in the scriptures helps us to counteract and conquer those things that want to stop or stunt us spiritually.

Paul's words in Philippians 3:13–14 have always been a help to me personally. He says,

> Brethren, I count not myself to have apprehended: but this one thing I do, forgetting those things which are behind, and reaching forth unto those things which are before, I press toward the mark for the prize of the high calling of God in Christ Jesus.

Paul had not taken hold of all that Christ had taken hold of him for. He was not all he wanted to be spiritually. In light of this, he had to forget about the past that could absorb or impede his progress and keep pressing toward the promises God had provided for him through Jesus Christ.

Pressing on and forgetting are key words that are good advice for all of us. This can be a starting point for a new direction and simply getting over it. Years ago when I taught a young adult Sunday school class, I remember telling the class that we would all be hurt or offended by others sooner or later. I also reminded us all that this could be either a stumbling stone or an opportunity for us to practice our faith. Just seeing things that happen to us as an opportunity instead of an offense can certainly put a person in a place of advantage in dealing with disappointments, hurts, or hard feelings.

For the last several years of my life, I have learned that a strong faith in the Lord can help us not only to see ourselves in a different way but to see others in a different way also. We all are capable of doing or saying things that can hurt us or hurt others. If we allow God's word to help identify who we really are and what we all deal with, namely a fallen nature, this can be a step in the right direction to a better understanding of why humanity acts the way it does. The good news is that God offers us a new nature by exercising faith in Jesus Christ. This can help counteract the dominance of the old nature. The point is this new nature or new man is what is so desperately needed as we deal with others and ourselves. Paul understood this truth better than most of us, when it comes to dealing with the old and new nature. He commented on these truths in Colossians 3:8–10.

> But now ye also put off all these; anger, wrath, malice, blasphemy, filthy communication out of your mouth. Lie not one to another, seeing that ye have put off the old man with his deeds; And have put on the new man, which is renewed in knowledge after the image of him that created him.

If one is willing to believe that God has provided a way for humankind to have a new nature and be willing to feed, nurture, and put on this new man daily, only good can come from it. God's way is a good fix for getting over it, on or off the golf course.

> Put on therefore, as the elect of
> God, holy and beloved,
> bowels of mercies, kindness, humbleness of mind,
> meekness and longsuffering; Forbearing one another,
> and forgiving one another, if any man have a
> quarrel against any; even as Christ forgave you,
> so also do ye.
> —Colossians 3:12–13

CHAPTER 50

Numbers

Numbers get a lot of attention in the game of golf. The success of the game hinges a lot on numbers. I was watching golf a few days ago, the shot came up short, and I noticed the player looking at the number on his club. The numbers on my golf clubs are not a problem to me; it's the ones on the scorecard that really get my attention.

Numbers are something that can cause a lot of problems and concerns in so many facets of life. After being so blessed to have worked and enjoyed a paycheck every week for fifty years, my wife and I find ourselves on a fixed income. Retirement is nice, but numbers are more important than ever to us now. When people ask me how I like retirement, I say, "My wife has twice the husband and half the paycheck." All joking aside, numbers do play such an important role in life. Sometimes we don't pay nearly enough attention to them. Days go by fast and time can run out. The apostle Paul talked about time when he wrote to the

Christians in Ephesus. In Ephesians 5:16, he talks about redeeming the time because the days are evil. I believe he was saying we need to take advantage of the opportunity given to us and make the most of it. I have written in my Bible a couple of quotes in relationship to this verse.4

1. Killing time murders opportunities.
2. Don't count the days. Make the days count.

A careful study of God's word shows over and over the importance of numbers. As I am writing this chapter I have been reading the book of Numbers. This book gives us the account of two numberings of the children of Israel. The first one was after they left Egypt. The second one occurred as they were nearing the end of their wandering in the wilderness for forty years before they would enter the Promised Land. Numbers are not only important to God but it is important that one takes the advice given in Psalm 90:10–12, where it says,

> The days of our years are threescore years and ten; and if by reason of strength they be fourscore years, yet is their strength labour and sorrow; for it is soon cut off, and we fly away. Who knoweth the power of thine anger? Even according to thy fear, so is thy wrath. So teach us to number our days, that we may apply our hearts unto wisdom.

The preceding verses in this psalm give a good comparison between God, who is everlasting to everlasting, and man, who is portrayed as weak, limited, and like grass that grows and flourishes but soon withers and is cut down. The psalmist, knowing how brief and unpredictable life is, encourages people, who may live to be seventy or eighty years old, to number their days. There are only so many days to apply our hearts to learn this wisdom, which comes from God.

Numbers do play a major role in our lives, so we all need to take advantage of them or they will take advantage of us.

Are not five sparrows sold for two farthings,
and not one of them is forgotten before God?
But even the very hairs of your head are numbered.
Fear not therefore: ye are of more value
than many sparrows.
—Luke 12:6–7

CHAPTER 51

The Trophy

The giving out of the prestigious claret jug and all the other trophies that we the spectators see while watching golf in our home is another enjoyable aspect of this game. I cannot imagine the emotion and satisfaction the golfers experience during this time. The presentation and the words spoken by the winners add to the climax of another tournament.

The one and only twenty inch tall trophy that I won fifty years ago still gets my attention once in awhile. It is not a fancy trophy and the good feeling of winning second place has faded, but most important, it is a reminder of a past achievement. Reminders can be such a positive thing in life that we all can take for granted. Our automobiles, appliances, smartphones, and numerous other things fall into this category. These reminders are put in place to make life safer and more convenient for us.

From the beginning of time, I think it is safe to say that reminders have been built into the very fabric of creation. From all the trees, vegetation, and plant life we can see these built-in reminders. My mother, Mildred Yoak, who is now deceased, took a seed from a peach and planted it years ago. That seed sprouted, grew into a tree, and eventually produced many delicious peaches over the years. I now live where that seed was first planted and every spring I start looking for buds and blooms on the tree, and it is a special reminder of my mother. All trees and vegetation that bud, bloom, and produce seeds should be a reminder of God's provisions for humanity as well as the animal life. The built-in reminder that God has created in the human body is also remarkable within itself.

Reminders can be painful in life but also very beneficial if they drive us to a deeper faith or a first-time faith in Christ who went to a cross and shed His blood to provide salvation to all who chooses to repent and believe in Him. The crosses that are so prevalent in dress today, on churches, and in cemeteries throughout the land certainly should be more than making a person, building, or grounds look good. I only hope these crosses remind us all of the sacrificial work of Christ who was willing to become sin for us so we could be made righteous in God's eyes. As one reads and studies the Bible, one cannot help but see the vocal reminders as well as the visible ones. In the very beginning of the New Testament, you see John the Baptist, the one who came to prepare the way for the Messiah. As one of the New Testament reminders, his message in Matthew 3:2 as well as the other gospels was to repent for the kingdom of God was at hand. He was reminding them there was a change that needed to be made if they would be a part of this kingdom.

In the Old Testament, we see all the prophets that God raised up to be vocal reminders to His chosen people, Israel, and the surrounding nations. In the Old Testament, you will also read about physical reminders designed to keep alive the memories of significant events that took place in the history of the nation of Israel. One of these physical reminders today, for the Jewish people, is the observance of the Passover that commemorates or keeps the memory alive in how God delivered the people from bondage in Egypt. This physical reminder parallels what believers in Christ do when they receive communion in their local churches. The believer is to do this in remembrance of Christ, our Passover, who was sacrificed for us. For the one who puts value in the message of God's word, you can only conclude that it is full of reminders.

While we all get enjoyment from and cherish our life achievements, I am reminded of the old gospel song that says,

On a hill far away stood an old rugged cross, The emblem of suffering and shame; And I love that old cross where the dearest and best For a world of lost sinners was slain. So I'll cherish the old rugged cross, Till my trophies at last I lay down;

I will cling to the old rugged cross, And exchange
it some day for a crown.[4]

Know ye not that they which run in a race run
all, but one receiveth the prize? So run, that
ye may obtain. And every man that striveth for
the mastery is temperate in all things. Now they
do it to obtain a corruptible crown; but we an
incorruptible. I therefore so run, not as uncertainly;
so fight I, not as one that beateth the air: But I
keep under my body, and bring it into subjection;
lest that by any means, when I have preached
to others, I myself should be a castaway.
—1 Corinthians 9:24–27

CHAPTER 52

Relationships

Recently while watching golf on television, I heard an announcer say, "There are fifty million golfers in the world." I do not know how they determine that statistic, but it is astonishing. It is even more amazing when one stops and thinks about all the social and economic benefits that have come to society because of this game. In this book, I have tried to bring out some of the other benefits of this game besides winning. One of these is the relationships that are developed and cultivated on the golf course. I think it is safe to say we somewhat develop a relationship with the players we get to watch on television, although it is not a personal one. The media can be the mode that connects us with the men and women who play on the professional level. Their level of play, sportsmanship, and the way they conduct themselves can strengthen this relationship with the viewers. On the other hand, personal relationships are such an important part of life. As I write this chapter, my family and I have just celebrated another

Thanksgiving together. The food and fellowship were great and the weather was beautiful. I could only say,

> Thank You, Lord. Besides, my brother and I are going golfing on Black Friday and that sure beats fighting the crowds in the busy stores. Let all the golfers say amen.

When I started this book over a year ago, it started on a personal note, and I would like to end it the same way. Since this chapter is about relationships, it is only appropriate for me to first talk about one that started over fifty years ago. This relationship is not about golf but about a girl named Darlene Collins who I met in high school, and it resulted in us getting married on July 18, 1964. From this relationship are a special son, Gary, and a beautiful daughter, Shelby, who is married to Jeff Nuckolls. They now have two daughters, Mikhaila and Sydney, and we have two beautiful granddaughters. They also have a Maltipoo named Molly that we call our "grand dog." Life is good, and family is at the top of the list. Of course, there have been difficulties in our family like most families have, but the enjoyment and blessings that we have had as a family, surely outweigh any bad.

From my point of view, my golfing relationships have also been an enjoyment and a blessing. The individuals that I have played golf with over the years have only made my golf experience more memorable. Therefore,

I feel it necessary that I recognize some of them in the acknowledgment section of this book.

Like most relationships there seems to be something that connects or fosters it. If that little nine-hole hillside golf course had never been built on the north side in Grantsville, West Virginia, I may never have developed a relationship with golf. It is always beneficial to look back on life's relationships and be thankful for those that have been good and made one a better person. Sometimes bad things in life can be the avenue for relationships. A good close friend, Bill Woods, died suddenly after surgery from a brain aneurysm, leaving a wife and three children. As bad and hurtful as this untimely death was to the family and all of us who knew Bill, it was used by the Lord to make me see myself and the uncertainty of life. It was at his funeral that I heard and realized that I needed a Savior. It was a turning point in my life that later resulted in me repenting of my sins and receiving Jesus Christ as my personal Savior. It was at that moment, although I did not fully understand it, that I now had a relationship with Jehovah God, my Creator and Savior. This relationship has made our family more complete and has given me a new outlook on life. Many years have passed since that day, and thousands of times I have turned the pages of the Bible, God's word, which has resulted in strengthening and knowing more about this relationship.

At that time in my life, I might have thought that I was coming to the Lord, when actually He was coming to me. We must all understand that God's word teaches us that sin severed the relationship between humans and their Creator. Because of this, Christ came into the world in a supernatural way to reconcile and restore humanity back to him. The word of God rings out loud and clear that He has done his part so that "whosoever" may come to Christ, if they choose to do so. Paul says it best in 2 Corinthians 5:18–19.

> And all things are of God, who hath reconciled us to himself by Jesus Christ, and hath given to us the ministry of reconciliation; To wit, that God was in Christ, reconciling the world unto himself, not imputing their trespasses unto them; and hath committed unto us the word of reconciliation.

These verses are so much about compounding a difference between humankind and God, which results in restoring a broken relationship. The reconciliation that God initiated in Christ has been committed now to humankind as we attempt to share the gospel message that Jesus saves. This reconciliation ministry need is driven by love, because that is what drove God to come to us in the person of Jesus Christ. Paul echoes this in Romans 5:8–10, when he says,

> But God commendeth his love toward us, in that,
> while we were yet sinners, Christ died for us.
> Much more then, being now justified by his blood,
> we shall be saved from wrath through him. For
> if, when we were enemies, we were reconciled to
> God by the death of his Son, much more, being
> reconciled, we shall be saved by his life.

God's greatest demonstration of love was shown to us sinners, when Jesus died and shed His blood for us so we could be reconciled to Him and escape the wrath to come.

The same way that physical relationships take a degree of faith, trust, and work to materialize and develop, it is no different with a spiritual relationship that is so needed by all in this uneven journey called life.

In the conclusion of this book, I must say if you have received Christ as Savior by faith, keep working on this most important relationship. This work does not save you; it simply helps you to stand strong against the many enemies that are out to undermine your faith. Paul tells the believers in Philippians 2:12 to work out your own salvation with fear and trembling. He does not say to work for your salvation but to work it out, because God has provided this free gift to all that will believe and receive Christ as their Savior. As believers, we need to work out our salvation by practicing the things that God's word tells us to do. Working out is important to make us strong physically, and it is the same spiritually.

If you have read this book and are following the Lord scripturally keep working on this most important relationship. If you have never trusted Christ to save you, I pray that something has been said in these pages that may awaken an interest in you for the word of God. It can show you the way to have a personal relationship with the Lord through Jesus Christ.

Come unto me, all ye that labour
and are heavy laden, and I will give you rest.
Take my yoke upon you, and learn of me;
for I am meek and lowly in heart:
and ye shall find rest unto your souls.
For my yoke is easy, and my burden is light.
—Matthew 11:28–30

Acknowledgments

I heard a quote years ago that not only had an impact on my life but also has been a reminder to me as I have interacted and tried to minister to and help others down through the years. The quote says, "People don't care how much you know until they know how much you care." This acknowledgment section is about those that I care about on the golf course and those who cared enough to help me in writing this book, including the following:

- my wife, Darlene, who was always so willing to listen and help get all of my handwritten material put in the computer
- my son, Gary, who made some important suggestions in the arrangement and publishing of this book
- my sister, Patricia Nedeff, for her suggestions and encouragement and for providing me with art supplies that I used in drawing a couple of pictures
- my son-in-law, Jeff, who was willing to proofread this book

- all on the PGA and LPGA that I so enjoy watching on the golf channel who have played a role in me writing a book
- all who encouraged and prayed for me while I was in the writing process
- the Lord, who has given me strength and inspiration to write this book
- all my golfing buddies that I have been blessed to know down through the years:
  - Frank Criss, a good, positive golfer who loves to play and sees more than the greens and fairways while playing.
  - Bob Sprout, a deep thinker with a dry sense of humor who is always willing to play.
  - Dan Martin, a brother in the Lord and fellow pastor whose determination to get across the water was quite humorous to his gallery. He can even put some humor into keeping score when he writes down those questionable nines.
  - Dave Gandee, a brother in the Lord that hits the ball great and is always encouraging others.
  - Ron Fleming, Stan Houchin, and Don Yeager, who invited me to go of a two-day golf outing. Ron is a good golfer and loves the game. His favorite saying on the course is "That's life in the big city." Stan, who is a Christian gentleman, made sure we had devotions each

night after our game. Don Yeager, who loves the game, told me one day that he had used in a sermon what I titled chapter 13—"Hole in One"—in this book. The "Whole in One" he was talking about is more important than the hole in one that I wrote about.

- Darrell Raines, a coworker and a hunting buddy that took up golf later in life. He enjoys laughing and having a good time while playing.
- Larry O'Neal, a good friend, pastor, and golfer who prayed with me the night I accepted the Lord as my Savior. Unbeknown to me, I would later pastor the church that he had pastored for fourteen years.
- Norvil Deem, who is now deceased, a good golfer who loved to play and always kept the game moving forward.
- Bud Hays, a gentleman always willing to play.
- Gary Conger, who always gets the Conger roll.
- Allan Poff, who always says sweet after a good shot.
- Rick Gant, a hard-hitting golfer and brother in the Lord who let me hit his graphite shaft clubs, which later inspired me to buy that kind.
- Harold Lemley, whose faith is contagious, always played the Good Samaritan Tournament. His son, Zack, was unable to

play, but his presence and smiles help make the tournament more enjoyable.

- Jeff Kisner, a good athlete who loves sports and coaching and can hit the ball a mile. We served the Lord together for many years at Faith Baptist Church.
- Bob Yoak, my biological brother and spiritual brother who plays golf with me sometimes at Myrtle Beach and locally. He is my best friend and has shown generosity to me many times.

These words that I have expressed here may be inadequate so it is only appropriate to end by saying, "Thank you!"

Endnotes

Word definitions are taken from *Strong's Exhaustive Concordance of the Bible* (Riverside Book and Bible House, Iowa Falls, Iowa) and *The Webster's II New Riverside University Dictionary* (The Riverside Publishing Company, 1984).

Chapter 4

[1] Footnote quoted from *The New Defender's Study Bible*, World Publishing, Nashville, Tennessee, 1995, 24, Genesis 3:21.

Chapter 7

[2] Quote taken from *Growing Strong in the Seasons of Life* by Chuck Swindoll, Multnomah Press, Portland, Oregon, 1983, 229.

Chapter 8

[1] Footnote quoted from *The New Defender's Study Bible*, World Publishing, Nashville, Tennessee, 1995, 17, Genesis 2:17.

Chapter 12

[1] Footnote quoted from *The New Defender's Study Bible*, World Publishing, Nashville, Tennessee, 1995, 1,564, John 1:14.

Chapter 16

[3] Golf joke taken from *The Treasure of Clean Jokes* by Tal D. Bonham, Broadman Press, Nashville, Tennessee, 1981, 137.

Chapter 17

[2] Quote taken from *Come before Winter and Share My Hope* by Chuck Swindoll, Tyndale House Publishers, Wheaton, Illinois, 1985, 169.

Chapter 47

[1] Footnote quoted from *The New Defender's Study Bible*, World Publishing, Nashville, Tennessee, 1995, 1,849, 1 Thessalonians 5:23.

Chapter 48

[4] Quote from *Favorite Hymns of Praise*, Tabernacle Publishing Company, Wheaton, Illinois, 1967, "Trust and Obey," 365.

Chapter 51

[4] Quote from *Favorite Hymns of Praise*, Tabernacle Publishing Company, Wheaton, Illinois, 1967, "The Old Rugged Cross," 317.

Printed in the United States
By Bookmasters